D1409009

A WOMAN'S PLACE
IS IN THE BOARDROOM
THE ROADMAP

Also by Peninah Thomson:

"Public sector human resource management: an agenda for change," in Michael Armstrong (ed.) *Strategies for Human Resource Management*, Kogan Page, 1992.

"Public sector management in a period of radical change 1979–1992," in Norman Flynn (ed.) *Change in the Civil Service: A Public Finance Foundation Reader*, The Chartered Institute of Public Finance and Accountancy, 1994.

"Aftermath: making public sector change work: Part I," *Public Policy Review*, **3**(1): 54–6, 1995.

"A paradigm shift: making public sector change work: Part II," *Public Policy Review*, **3**(2): 60–4, 1995.

The Changing Culture of Leadership: Women Leaders' Voices, Elizabeth Coffey, Clare Huffington and Peninah Thomson, The Change Partnership, 1999.

"Making the case for business: the change agenda," in *Work-Life Strategies for the 21st Century*, report by the National Work-Life Forum, 2000.

"Introduction," in Elizabeth Coffey and colleagues from The Change Partnership, *10 Things That Keep CEOs Awake and How to Put Them to Bed*, McGraw-Hill, 2003.

"Corporate governance, leadership and culture change in business", a lecture with Mark Goyder and John Roberts, Royal Society of Arts, 2003.

A Woman's Place is in the Boardroom, with Jacey Graham and Tom Lloyd, Palgrave Macmillan, 2005.

"The FTSE 100 Cross-Company Mentoring Programme," in Thérèse Torris (ed.) *Mentoring – A Powerful Tool for Women*, Women@Work No.7, Publications@EuropeanPWN.net, 2007.

"Being on a Board," in Mirella Visser and Annalisa Gigante (eds) *Women on Boards: Moving Mountains*, Women@Work No.8, Publications@EuropeanPWN. net, 2007.

Also by Jacey Graham:

"Shell Oil Company US: the 2004 Catalyst award winner for diversity initiatives," with Leslie Mays and Susan Vinnicombe, in Cary Cooper (ed.) *Supporting Women's Career Advancement: Challenges and Opportunities*, Edward Elgar, 2005.

A Woman's Place is in the Boardroom, with Peninah Thomson and Tom Lloyd, Palgrave Macmillan, 2005.

"Diversity & inclusion: moving to the next level," with Lesley Brook, in Joy Iverson (ed.) *Diverse Britain: The Changing Face of a Nation*, St James's House, 2008.

Also by Tom Lloyd:

Dinosaur & Co.: *Studies in Corporate Evolution*, RKP, 1984; Penguin, 1985.

Managing Knowhow, with Karl-Erik Sveiby, Bloomsbury, 1987.

The Nice Company, Bloomsbury, 1990; Calmann-Levy, France, 1992; FrancoAngeli, Italy, 1993.

Entrepreneur!, Bloomsbury, 1992.

The Charity Business, John Murray, 1993.

A Woman's Place is in the Boardroom, with Peninah Thomson and Jacey Graham, Palgrave Macmillan, 2005.

A WOMAN'S PLACE IS IN THE BOARDROOM

THE ROADMAP

PENINAH THOMSON
AND JACEY GRAHAM

WITH TOM LLOYD

palgrave
macmillan

First published 2008 by
PALGRAVE MACMILLAN
Houndmills, Basingstoke, Hampshire RG21 6XS and
175 Fifth Avenue, New York, N.Y. 10010
Companies and representatives throughout the world

PALGRAVE MACMILLAN is the global academic imprint of the Palgrave
Macmillan division of St. Martin's Press, LLC and of Palgrave Macmillan Ltd.
Macmillan® is a registered trademark in the United States, United Kingdom
and other countries. Palgrave is a registered trademark in the European
Union and other countries.

ISBN-13: 978–0–230–53712–5
ISBN-10: 0–230–53712–X

This book is printed on paper suitable for recycling and made from fully
managed and sustained forest sources. Logging, pulping and manufacturing
processes are expected to conform to the environmental regulations of the
country of origin.

A catalogue record for this book is available from the British Library.

A catalog record for this book is available from the Library of Congress.

10 9 8 7 6 5 4 3 2 1
17 16 15 14 13 12 11 10 09 08

Printed in Great Britain by
Cromwell Press Ltd, Trowbridge, Wiltshire

For aspiring women directors everywhere, and for all those who are architects of corporate change

CONTENTS

LIST OF ILLUSTRATIONS, TABLES AND FIGURES

Illustrations

Tables

Figures

PREFACE

Although it did not seem that way at the time, *A Woman's Place is in the Boardroom* wasn't a one-off intervention, but the first step on a journey. This book is the second. Our purpose – to use our ideas and experience to help able women to become credible candidates for positions on corporate boards – remains the same. But in the three years since the first book was published, we have become even more convinced that the general problem we're trying to address, the absence of women from top strategic decision-making bodies, is among the most important problems of our time. We suggested in our Preface to the earlier book that "the problems that face our world are so complex and difficult that we will need all the talent available to solve them." There can be no doubt that progress has been made since then, in terms of the representation of women on boards, but nor can there be much doubt that the complexity and difficulty of the issues and problems we face have also increased.

Since 2005, we have had the "July bombings" in London and many other acts of terrorism; pressure on world resources has grown; we've all become much more aware of the impact of climate change; the world's financial system has endured the credit crunch, which at the time of writing was still being billed as heralding a potential recession; political, social and economic problems in the Middle East, Asia and Africa have proliferated; and a whole series of natural and man-made disasters in other parts of the world have haunted the headlines.

More women on the boards of our large companies isn't going to solve any of these problems at a stroke, of course, but it will contribute to their solution, by increasing the reservoirs of human ingenuity, imagination, insight and *will* available to address them. We believe that in the final analysis, it's what you *do* with power and influence that matters. In another turbulent age, John Donne (1572–1631) wrote:

> No man is an Island, entire of itself; every man is a piece of the Continent, a part of the main; if a clod be washed away by the sea, Europe is the less, as well as if a promontory were, as well as if a manor of thy friend's or of thine own were; any man's death diminishes me, because I am involved in Mankind. (Meditation XVII)

If this book can help in a small way to ensure that more women with intelligence of both kinds (both EQ and IQ), who are able, competent, experienced, strong-willed, committed to civil values, possessed of some vision and good judgment, and eager to apply their qualities to solving the problems that we all face, attain positions of authority and influence, it will have been worth writing.

PENINAH THOMSON AND JACEY GRAHAM

The authors can be contacted at:

Peninah.thomson@Praesta.com   Jacey.graham@brookgraham.com
www.praesta.com   www.brookgraham.com

Acknowledgements

Donne said: "No man is an island." No woman is an island either and especially not when writing a book. Or any rate, we were not islands while writing this book. There are far too many people we would like to thank for their contributions and support to mention here, but we want to express our gratitude to some of them.

First, we remain extremely grateful for the continuing commitment and support of all the chairmen and CEOs who are mentors on the FTSE 100 Cross-Company Mentoring Programme and whose names appear in Table 1.1. In particular we would like to thank the following group of chairmen who've been with us from the start of this journey, who continue to provide much valued advice and challenge whenever we ask for it and who have shared their insights with readers at the beginning of each chapter: Roger Carr – chairman, Centrica plc; Sir Philip Hampton – chairman, J Sainsbury plc; Baroness Hogg – chairman, 3i plc; Sir Richard Evans – chairman, United Utilities plc; Sir Rob Margetts CBE, FrEng – chairman, Legal & General plc; Sir Mark Moody-Stuart KCMG – chairman, Anglo American plc; Richard Olver FrEng – chairman, BAE Systems plc; Sir John Parker – chairman, National Grid plc; David Reid – chairman, Tesco plc; and Paul Skinner – chairman, Rio Tinto plc.

We are also grateful for the contributions of many current and former mentees on the program who have helped us to distil our thoughts into what we call the "roadmap," which provides the structure of this book. Their insights and experience (sometimes positive, sometimes painful) have helped shape what we hope will prove a useful guide for other women.

We have benefited greatly from our discussions about director development with Krister Svensson. The requests we have received for help in establishing programs of the same kind as the FTSE 100 Cross-Company Mentoring Programme, and the many interesting conversations that followed, have also helped to hone our thinking and our approach to developing the UK program. So thanks also to Anne Bouverot, Avivah Wittenberg-Cox, Thérèse Torris, Véronique Préaux-Cobi and Eva Bernecke, Julie Avrane-Chopard, Mary Meaney, Stephanie MacKendrick, Thea Miller, Annalisa Gigante, and Mirella Visser. We would also like to thank Alison Maitland.

Several search firms are now working with us in support of the program. They have taken time to meet some of our mentees, to promote the diversity of shortlists to their clients, and have helped us develop a deeper understanding of the issues and the potential solutions. Our express thanks go to: Julia Budd at Zygos; Ffion Hague at Hanson Green; Giles Crewdson at Korn/Ferry; Philip Marsden and Rachael Erskine at Ridgeway Partners; and Patricia Tehan. Spencer Stuart in London has kindly given places on its directors' program to several mentees. Thanks too to Julie Daum at Spencer Stuart in New York, for keeping us informed about board developments in the Fortune 500. In terms of ongoing research, our thanks to Professor Susan Vinnicombe OBE, Dr. Val Singh and their colleagues at the International Centre for Women Leaders, Cranfield School of Management, and to Ilene Lang and colleagues at Catalyst, New York.

JPMorgan has allowed us to describe the development workshops we co-designed with Betsy Nelson and the retention team at the investment bank. Our thanks go to Klaus Diederichs, head of investment banking coverage in Europe, and to Bill Winters, Co-CEO of the investment bank.

Praesta Partners LLP has sponsored the FTSE 100 Cross-Company Mentoring Programme from its inception, and without the firm's commitment there would be no story to tell. We thank all the partners for their support. Our particular thanks to Mairi Eastwood and Philip Graf for their unfailing enthusiasm for "the project"; to Hilary Lines for her ideas, challenges and input, as we developed the program and while we were writing, and to Hazel Devery for her speed, efficiency and accuracy, which have proved invaluable throughout the project. At Brook Graham LLP, we would like to thank Lesley Brook for allowing space to tackle a second volume of *A Woman's Place is in the Boardroom*, for her continuing support of the program and her expertise as a sounding board. A big thank you to Jane Harris for her insights on the political model that is used so successfully in our work with women and which we describe briefly in Chapter 2. Other contributors without whom this book would be a lesser work are Professor Bob Garratt of Cass Business School, who provided many insights on corporate governance and designed the governance self-test that appears in Chapter 3. Baroness Fritchie, Stephen Brenninkmeyer and Anne Watts OBE, the members of our Advisory Council, have helped us to envision the directions in which the FTSE 100 Cross-Company Mentoring Programme might develop.

Many of the people who supported us in the production of the first book have continued to do so: we would particularly like to thank Barbara Shore for her cartoons, and Stephen Rutt, our publisher at Palgrave Macmillan.

Stephen encouraged us to write this second book, and he and his team have been a consistent source of guidance and enthusiasm.

Finally, we could never have embarked on this project without knowing that we would have the unstinting support of those nearest and dearest to us. You know who you are and we thank you for your unfailing interest, patience and encouragement.

Every effort has been made to trace all the copyright holders, but if any have been inadvertently overlooked the publishers will be pleased to make the necessary arrangements at the first opportunity.

We thought we had said it all in our first book, *A Woman's Place is in the Boardroom*. We analyzed the figures on female directors on boards. We explained why the gender imbalance on boards was a problem for businesses. Through dozens of interviews with male chairmen, female directors, women who aspire to main board positions and headhunters, we revealed how the imbalance was perceived by all those implicated in it, and affected by it. We summarized all the evidence and arguments in the academic literature. We broke the problem down into its component causes and we suggested ways to address each component in a concerted effort to achieve a better gender balance on boards.

But our readers wanted more. They accepted the evidence and analysis and they were persuaded by the argument, but they wanted more on the "how to." Thanks to our continued involvement in the FTSE 100 Cross-Company Mentoring Programme – it goes from strength to strength, and is being emulated in several other countries – we've learned a great deal since the publication of the original book in 2005. We've also developed some new ideas and tools, including what's proving to be a useful matrix of the problem's important dimensions.

So here is the extended "how to" derived from what we've learned. We call it a "roadmap." It sets out the route that women executives who want to improve their chances of being appointed to boards should follow and the signs, signals and points to note along the way. We hope the book will also be useful to companies wishing to appoint more female directors.

We are dealing with a market here. On the demand side are companies seeking suitable and suitably qualified executive and non-executive directors. On the supply side there are suitable, suitably qualified women willing and eager to test their mettle in the boardroom.

Sometimes it seems the other way round; that women are seeking board positions that companies supply. The perception is understandable in individual cases. Women who have been applying, unsuccessfully, for executive and non-executive directorships for some years naturally see unwilling suppliers. This is a misperception. The shortage is of qualified candidates, not of board vacancies. Several variables may affect the balance of supply and demand at any one time. At present, demand is being affected, negatively, by a slight reduction in board size, and, positively, by a reduction in the number of directorships it's deemed appropriate (by modern corporate governance policies and codes of practice) for an individual to hold. The demand for female directors in particular is increasing, because of the desire of many companies for more diversity on their boards.

The nub of the problem is that women are not contributing as much to addressing the shortage of qualified candidates for board positions as their representation in junior and middle management levels would lead one to expect.

There are two possible explanations for this; first, gender-specific inadequacies in women candidates, perceived or real; second, general inadequacies in director selection processes. (Insofar as the former are more perceived than real, the supply and demand problems are, of course, related, but it's usual and we think useful to consider them separately, at least initially.) Our experience so far with the FTSE 100 Cross-Company Mentoring Programme suggests it is a bit of both; that women aren't sufficiently well prepared for board positions and that companies can and should do more to steer their senior women in the right directions.

In our earlier book, we argued that these supply and demand factors should be addressed at the same time; that there is much that women can and should do to improve their chances of becoming directors and that there's also much that companies can and should do both to make themselves more attractive to women seeking board positions and to remove the cultural, psychological and organizational obstacles that deter them from appointing more women to their boards. Our approach in this book follows this twin-track method.

This is a practical book. We take it as the conventional wisdom that companies need to appoint more women to their boards, and we propose measures and approaches that women and companies can take that could help both to achieve their respective goals. We showed, in the first book, that there's common ground here. Most of the male chairmen and senior executives we speak to want to attract and keep more female executives, and to appoint the most able to their boards. We have no reason to suppose they were lying or telling us what they thought we wanted to hear, rather than what they really believe. The number of chairmen and chief executives (CEOs) who've signed up to be mentors in the FTSE 100 Cross-Company Mentoring Programme corroborates our belief that most leaders of large, UK companies want to appoint more women to their boards.

The problem is not incompatibility of female ambitions and corporate needs; it is a market inefficiency, more evident in some companies than in others. To help our female readers to assess their readiness for board membership and to help companies to assess their readiness to take the next vital step in the evolution of corporate governance towards gender-balanced boards, we have included reader exercises at the end of some chapters.

Before that, however, we will begin in Chapter 1, The state of play, by summarizing the latest statistics for women on boards in the UK and the US, describing the origins and current status of the FTSE 100 Cross-Company Mentoring Programme, briefly describing a few initiatives and projects it has inspired elsewhere, and introducing the "roadmap." This sets out in matrix form eight main challenges that we and the program's mentors believe female executives confront in their campaigns to become credible candidates for board appointments and the steps they can take to meet those challenges.

The roadmap has already proved useful to ambitious women aspiring to, and preparing themselves for, high corporate office. We believe that it could prove equally useful to company leaders who see women as a substantial, still largely untapped source of board-level management talent. The challenge for companies is in many ways the mirror image of the challenge for women, as both sides of the market endeavor to make the boardroom common ground. The shape of this book is based on the roadmap and its mirror.

In Chapter 2, Deciding to engage, we focus on the decision all women executives must make – consciously or by default – of whether or not to throw their hats into the ring, and declare themselves contenders for board positions. We discuss the factors they will need to take into account when reaching their decision, emphasize the need to be alert and decisive, and pay particular attention to the issue that, in our experience, is of most concern to board-minded women; namely, whether they're committed enough to stomach the corporate politics.

Chapter 3, The written rules of engagement, will set out, in general terms, the formal framework within which all directors operate: the structure of boards, including the board committee system; the legal roles and duties of directors; basic, board-level finance; a listed company's relationship with capital markets, its investors, lenders, and so on – what we call the "board basics." This chapter is not supposed to be a tutorial, but rather a list of areas with which you need to be familiar before you can make a rational decision to engage, and start to work towards becoming a credible board candidate. We suggest ways in which to acquire these insights into the formal framework in which a board operates and how companies can help and encourage their female executives to "get up to speed" in modern corporate governance.

The board basics constitute the formal framework and language of the board. In Chapter 4, The unwritten rules, we focus on the informal group dynamics of the "board milieu" (the board itself and the areas around it peopled by those close to and approaching it). Once you've "decided to engage" and have familiarized yourself with the formal rules, you should study the social dynamics of the board milieu and try to understand how your personality and gender will affect them, so that you can begin to acclimatize yourself, rationally and emotionally, to the idea of being a director.

In Chapter 5, A sense of direction, we will argue that women need to set themselves some provisional goals, and describe how to identify industries that interest them and interesting companies within those industries where their chances of board appointments seem relatively high. We will recommend that they regard their strategic targets and tactical sub-targets as provisional and suggest that one implication of such targeting for company leaders who want to appoint women to their boards is that it's in their interests to make their companies particularly interesting for able women with board ambitions.

Authentic, easy-to-be-with, personable and visible personalities are appointed to boards, not people masquerading as their conceptions of an ideal director, who are "hard work" socially, one dimensional, or timid. To be a credible board candidate you must put yourself about a bit, raise your head above the parapet, make an impression, and earn respect, while remaining true to yourself, and your values and beliefs. When you raise your profile in this way, you create an image in the minds of other people. This image is what you take to market in informal soundings, formal interviews and presentations of various kinds. In Chapter 6, Cultivating board qualities, we discuss how to raise your profile, and create the kind of image that says to the powers that be that you are board material.

"If you fail to plan, you plan to fail" is as true for women bidding for board appointments as it is for any other business endeavor. We explain in Chapter 7, Setting out your stall, how to put together a personal marketing plan and draft a personal marketing document. We describe its components and identify the constituencies at which it should be aimed. A company also needs plans and policies if its wish for a more gender-balanced board is to be realized. We describe the kinds of plans it needs, including plans for seeding its pipeline of board candidates with more women, and so increasing the chances that its next board appointment will be a woman.

An advantage of the goal-setting process we describe in Chapter 5 is that it highlights the current gaps and areas of weakness you need to make good, to become a credible board candidate. If your personal marketing document describes you as you are now, you can deduce from your targets a picture of you as you need to become, if you're to be a credible candidate for a board appointment. In Chapter 8, Mind the gap, we discuss the role of feedback and reflection in achieving the self-awareness you will need to identify gaps and weaknesses, stress the importance of remaining authentic while changing, and explain why you need to broaden your horizons and consider the bigger picture at board level.

Since there's no substitute for experience, the best preparation for joining a board is serving as an executive or non-executive director on a subsidiary company board, or the board of another organization, such as a small non-competing company in the FTSE 250, or a charity. In Chapter 9, Board games, we discuss how to secure such positions, the kinds of positions women should look for and how they can use the experience to increase their chances of gaining an appointment to a main board. Company leaders can help here by encouraging, sponsoring and recommending their female high-fliers when they apply for these "junior" board appointments, and using their networks to keep a lookout for suitable vacancies.

In the concluding chapter, Over the horizon, we will speculate about the future – for women on boards and for the FTSE 100 Cross-Company Mentoring Programme – and summarize the conclusions reached during a dinner towards the end of 2007, at which mentors and mentees on the program and several headhunters discussed what more they could do to improve the gender balance on corporate boards.

Progress, in terms of numbers, remains slow, but the issue is out in the open. The seeds have been sown and they're growing in the light. Companies in all industries are engaged now on the new gender front in the war for talent, and are trying hard to attract and keep able women. It will take a while for the pipelines to fill, but if senior female executives and companies heed the prescriptions and advice we set out in this book, we believe that the numbers of women on the boards of UK companies should rapidly start to increase.

CHAPTER 1

The state of play

There is a chicken and egg situation – to get more women on boards we need more women in senior executive positions, but equally having women on boards helps to accelerate that process. Business needs to use all available talent effectively.

Sir Mark Moody-Stuart, chairman, Anglo American plc

When the story of the gender balancing of main boards is written 100 years from now, 2006 will be seen as a minor hesitation in the march of women to their rightful position of parity with men.

It didn't seem that way in early 2007. There was more than a hint of frustration in the latest report by Catalyst, an American non-profit organization focusing on women's issues, on the proportion of women on the boards of America's largest listed companies. "At the current rate of change," the report's authors cried impatiently, "it will take women 73 years to reach parity with men in the boardrooms of Fortune 500 companies."[1]

Catalyst's survey showed that women board members as a percentage of all the directors of Fortune 500 companies fell marginally from 14.7 percent in 2005 to 14.6 percent in 2006. And the number of companies with no women directors at all rose a fraction.

A similar picture of stagnation verging on decline in the proportion of female directors of UK companies emerged from Cranfield University's *The Female FTSE Report 2006*. Female-held directorships at the UK's 100 largest listed companies fell from 121 (10.5 percent) in 2005 to 117 (10.35 percent) in 2006. FTSE 100 companies had one more female executive director in 2006, bringing the total to 15. They lost five female non-executive directors, however, and the number of companies with no female directors rose from 22 to 23.[2]

In its swansong report, the UK Equal Opportunities Commission (EOC), since replaced by the Commission for Equality and Human Rights, calculated that it would take another 65 years to achieve gender parity in FTSE 100 boardrooms. The implied suggestion that the UK will overtake the US at some stage in the next 50 years emerged from trend analysis. Although the UK numbers were lower, they had been rising faster over the previous five years.[3]

For those who believe, as we do, that everyone (investors, employees and society at large) will benefit when there are more women at the top of our largest companies, the 2006 figures were not encouraging. But nor should they have been seen as particularly discouraging. A one-year dip does not make a trend and the long-term momentum was, as the next year's figures would show, still in the right direction. As always, the media and commentators made too much of the decline in the 2006 figures. It was disappointing that the proportion of women on the boards of the leading US and UK companies fell, but the 14.6 percent for Fortune 500 boards in 2006 compared with 9.6 percent in 1995 when Catalyst began tracking the figures, and the 10.35 percent for FTSE 100 boards in 2006 compared with under 6 percent in 1999 when Cranfield started its series of annual surveys.

The minor falls in the number of women on the boards of large US and the UK companies were both well within the scope of normal variation around the trend. Apart from confirming what we already knew, that the gender balancing of company boards is an extremely slow process, they told us little about the underlying situation. The Catalyst and EOC projections of time to parity were misleading, because they were based on the 2006 figures and the 2006 figures did not represent, as Catalyst suggested, "the current rate of change." One year's figures are tips of icebergs; the statistical consequences of complex blends of actions, decisions, pressures, adaptations, reports, comments and choices that came together years ago.

With such small populations, progress will inevitably be in fits and starts. The numbers may fall one year, and surge ahead the following year as they get back on trend. Just as too much shouldn't have been made of the lower numbers in Cranfield's *Female FTSE Report 2006*, so it would be premature to bill the *Female FTSE Index and Report 2007*, subtitled *A Year of Encouraging Progress*, as a breakthrough in the gender balancing of the leadership of UK plc.

There were some striking headlines in Cranfield's 2007 report. The number of women on FTSE 100 boards reached 100 for the first time; and female-held FTSE 100 directorships, at 123 (some women hold more than one), the proportion of total FTSE directorships held by women, at 11 percent, the number of female non-executive directors (NEDs), at 110, and the number of FTSE 100 boards with more than one female director, at 35, all recorded new highs. But improvements were not evident on all fronts. The number of companies with female executive directors, at 11, was below the 2002 figure (12) and the number without any female directors (24) was the highest since 2004.[4]

The figures did represent a welcome return to trend, however, and as the report's authors pointed out, there's some evidence of gathering momentum. Thirty women were appointed directors in 2007. That was a fifth of all new board appointments – the highest proportion since Cranfield started monitoring the Female FTSE in 1999. Five women had not previously held FTSE 100 directorships. More importantly for the pipeline, particularly for the number of female executive directors likely to be appointed in the near future, 122 women sat on FTSE 100 executive committees, an increase of 40 percent on 2006.

The US figures are also back on trend after the 2006 dip. Catalyst's 2007 census showed a small increase in the percentage of Fortune 500 directorships held by women, from 14.6 percent in 2006 (down from 14.7 percent in 2005) to 14.8 percent. The report also revealed that women chaired a higher percentage of powerful Fortune 500 board committees in 2007.[5]

The numbers are unlikely to falter significantly in the coming years. The issue of women on company boards is more alive today than it has ever been and – thanks partly, we like to think, to our arguments in our first book – it is now firmly established as a business issue, rather than a social equity issue.

We're still in the early stages of adaptation to the Higgs and Tyson reports, the debate on corporate governance, the systematic scrutiny of women on boards (by Catalyst and Cranfield and others), the publication of books such as ours and, more recently, Sylvia Ann Hewlett's *Off-Ramps and On-Ramps*[6] and, in the UK, the FTSE 100 Cross-Company Mentoring Programme.

And there are other signs that the pipeline is filling up.

In the UK at least, the omens for the figures over the next few years are encouraging. In addition to that sharp increase in the number of women on executive committees noted in *The Female FTSE Report 2007*, a survey of UK managers and senior executives in summer 2007 by the Chartered Management Institute and Remuneration Economics found that women accounted for 36 percent of managers and directors, compared with 31 percent in 2006. They were paid less than men, but that was partly because they were promoted earlier. The average age of female team leaders was 37, against 42 for male leaders. Female department heads were 40, on average, compared with 43 for men, and the average age of female directors was 44, compared with 48 for male directors. The female resignation rate was 7.8 percent in 2007. That was higher than the previous year's 5.7 percent, but the male resignation rate rose faster, from 4 percent to 6.4 percent, which suggests there was no significant gender component in the increase.[7]

Performance

As we suggested in our first book, the most powerful stimulus for the appointment of more women to boards would be clear, incontrovertible evidence that it led to improved corporate performance. We quoted a 2004 Catalyst study that found a significant correlation between the gender diversity of top teams at the 353 Fortune 500 companies that disclose diversity data. The top quartile, in gender diversity, outperformed the bottom quartile by 35 percent on return on equity, and 34 percent on total shareholder returns.[8]

Catalyst has since published another study looking at boards, rather than top teams. It showed that companies with three or more women on their boards outperformed the average even more significantly.[9] The new study divided Fortune 500 companies into four, according to the number of women on their boards. It found that, on average, the top quartile (those with the most women) outperformed the bottom by 53 percent on return on equity, 42 percent on return on sales and 66 percent on return on invested capital.

Another study by the world's leading strategy consultants McKinsey & Co. found that "companies where women are most strongly represented at board or top management level are also the companies that perform best." The McKinsey study ranked European listed companies according to the number and proportion of women on their executive committees, their function (CEOs/CFOs were given more weight than communications managers, for example) and the number of women on the board. The top ranked 89 companies outperformed their sectors in terms of return on equity (11.4 percent, against an average of 10.3 percent), earnings before interest and tax (11.1 percent against 5.8 percent) and stock price growth (64 percent against 47 percent, over the period 2005–07).[10] The McKinsey report noted that markets were taking a keen interest in gender diversity:

> investment funds such as CalPERS [the California Public Employees' Retirement System – the world's largest pension fund] in the US and Amazone in Europe include this indicator among their investment criteria.

An interesting correspondence between the McKinsey results, based on European companies, and the results of the second Catalyst study of US Fortune 500 companies is that both found the performance benefit kicks in "once a certain critical mass is attained: namely at least three women on management committees for an average membership of 10 people," as the McKinsey report puts it. The second Catalyst study found a "notably stronger-than-average performance at companies with three or more women board directors." The McKinsey report quoted the director of a bank:

> When women sit on an executive committee, the nature of interactions changes … but one woman there is not enough – you need several of them.

If one woman is a token and two's company (as Mrs Wintringham found in Britain's House of Commons; see Chapter 2), it seems that three's a competitive advantage.

As we pointed out in our first book, the fact of correlation doesn't necessarily imply causation. The correlations could be explained in various ways. Perhaps it's simply chance (that's unlikely, after the corroborations of the first Catalyst result provided by the McKinsey study and the second Catalyst study), or good performance and gender diversity could both be related to some other variable, such as size or enlightened management (maybe). It is possible, however, that the correlation is because companies that see women as a major, untapped source of management talent will tend, other things being equal, to assemble higher quality management teams (very probably); or because women are better managers than men (perhaps, see our first book*);* or because companies run by men *and* women are better run than companies run by men *or* women (almost certainly).

Whatever the reasons for the correlation, the fact that attention is being paid to gender diversity in top management teams by institutes and universities, and particularly by strategy consultants and major fund managers, is bound to concentrate the minds of companies, and their boards and nomination committees (Nomcos). So too is the press comment attracted by gender/performance studies, the annual rankings of companies by the gender balance of their board published by Catalyst and Cranfield School of Management and, not least, press coverage of the FTSE 100 Cross-Company Mentoring Programme.

In December 2007, Luxottica, Italian sunglasses maker, owner of Ray-Ban, and licensed maker and seller of such brands as Prada, Chanel and Versace, announced that it wanted 30 percent of its top 200 jobs to be held by women by 2009. Nicola Pelà, the company's HR director, said there were "compelling reasons why Luxottica should have more women at the top of the organisation." He mentioned three reasons in an interview with the *Financial Times.* First, about 60 percent of the company's customers were women. Second, recent research revealed that fund managers gave diversity substantial weightings when making decisions. Third, the luxury goods business is driven by innovation, and Pelà says: "The more diverse you are, the more likely you are to be innovative."[11]

(See Chapter 2 for a summary of research confirming the link between innovation and diversity.)

Origins of the FTSE 100 Cross-Company Mentoring Programme

The idea of the program was born in November 2003 at an off-the-record breakfast meeting at the Shell Centre in London. The gathering was convened by Women Directors on Boards – a UK Consortium for Action and Change, a campaign group, since disbanded after it had served its purpose, which the authors had been instrumental in assembling. Sir Philip Watts, at that time the chairman of Shell, and Patricia Hewitt, the then UK secretary of state for trade and industry, issued invitations to the chairmen of all FTSE 100 companies to attend.

The 17 chairmen who attended the meeting, and the 8 who couldn't make it, but had wanted to, said they were also concerned about the lack of women on UK boards and wanted to help correct the imbalance. We were somewhat surprised, at the time, by their unanimity and their eagerness to help.

When the conversation turned to practicalities, the idea of a cross-company secondment scheme for senior female executives was suggested and discussed. On reflection, however, the chairmen decided that it was impractical, because the kind of women they would be inclined to put forward for secondment to fellow FTSE 100 companies would be too valuable to be away from their businesses for any length of time. We were keen to harness their obvious enthusiasm, however, and when the discussion turned to the possibility that they could act as mentors of each other's senior women executives, we realized this idea could work. The FTSE 100 Cross-Company Mentoring Programme was the result.

After we had taken more soundings and consulted more widely, we began recruiting mentors and drafted some criteria (quite loose initially) for selecting our mentees. We won commitments from seven chairmen to become mentors, matched the pioneer mentors with senior women their peers had nominated, and drafted some guidelines to help mentors and mentees to get started (see Appendix). The FTSE 100 Cross-Company Mentoring Programme was launched in late 2004. Alison Maitland, then of the *Financial Times*, described it as "a ground-breaking programme to increase female representation in the boardroom."[12]

By 2007, 30 chairmen and CEOs, including some eminent executives not on FTSE 100 boards, such as Dominic Casserley, managing director of McKinsey UK and Ireland, Lord Currie, chairman of Ofcom, and Mark

Otty, chairman of Ernst & Young, were actively mentoring. Some were on their second or third mentees. Table 1.1 provides a full list of mentors at the time of writing.

TABLE 1.1 **FTSE 100 Cross-Company Mentoring Programme: mentors**		
Name	**Title**	**Company**
Sanjiv Ahuja	Chairman	Orange SA
Donald Brydon CBE	Chairman	Smiths Group plc
Roger Carr	Chairman	Centrica plc
Dominic Casserley	Managing Partner, UK & Ireland	McKinsey & Company Inc.
Patrick Cescau	CEO	Unilever plc
Lord Currie	Chairman	Ofcom
Mervyn Davies CBE	Chairman	Standard Chartered plc
Peter Erskine	Chairman and CEO	Telefonica O2 Europe plc
Sir Richard Evans CBE	Chairman	United Utilities plc
Iain Ferguson CBE	CEO	Tate & Lyle plc
Niall Fitzgerald KBE	Chairman	Reuters plc
Thomas Glocer	CEO	Reuters plc
Stephen Green	Chairman	HSBC Holdings plc
Anthony Habgood	Chairman	Whitbread Group plc and Bunzl plc
Sir Philip Hampton	Chairman	J Sainsbury plc
Baroness Hogg	Chairman	3i Group plc
David Kappler	Chairman	Premier Foods plc
Sir David Lees	Chairman	Tate & Lyle plc
Sir Rob Margetts CBE FREng	Chairman	Legal & General plc
Sir Tom McKillop	Chairman	Royal Bank of Scotland plc
Charles Miller Smith	Chairman	ScottishPower plc
Sir Mark Moody-Stuart KCMG	Chairman	Anglo American plc
Richard Olver FrEng	Chairman	BAE Systems plc
Mark Otty	Chairman	Ernst & Young
Sir John Parker FrEng	Chairman	National Grid plc
David Reid	Chairman	Tesco plc
Paul Skinner	Chairman	Rio Tinto plc
James Smith	Chairman	Shell UK Limited
Lord Dennis Stevenson	Chairman	HBOS plc
Peter Sutherland KCMG	Chairman	BP plc

Evolution

The inclusion in the program of some distinguished businesspeople who aren't chairmen or CEOs of FTSE 100 companies is an illustration of how the program has evolved over the past three years since its launch. Its name is becoming less of a description now and more of a brand. This is inevitable and, we believe, healthy. The constituents of the FTSE 100 change regularly, for one thing, as company fortunes wax and wane; mergers, acquisitions and disposals change the market capitalization pecking order; and private equity funds take companies private for the restructuring and reform programs they use to add value, prior to relisting. The chairmen of new entrants to the FTSE 100 are obvious candidates for the program, and sometimes approach us about joining, but it would be foolish, in our view, to dispense with the services of able and distinguished mentors simply because their companies leave the FTSE 100 for one reason or another or they move to another company outside the FTSE 100.

The globalization process, which can lead to changes in domicile and market of primary listing, is also encouraging us to look beyond the FTSE 100 for our mentors and mentees. (In idle moments we ponder the possibility that an international network of programs of this kind could emerge; see Chapter 10.) We are also more conscious now that there are many talented women going places, and many successful men able and eager to help them in the professional services, public and not-for-profit sectors, as well as in the corporate sector. In other words, our horizons for the program have widened.

The objective of the program now is to help female executives from the so-called "marzipan" layer (within two levels of the main board, or its equivalent) of large companies or organizations of comparable size, who are nominated by their chairmen (or equivalent), to secure appointments as executive or non-executive directors (NEDs) of large companies or equivalent positions in other large organizations.

The mentoring process

In our mentoring guidelines (see Appendix), we say that mentoring relationships work best when:

- based on mutual respect, candor and trust

- a mentee gives her mentor a clear idea of what she's hoping to gain

- the parties commit themselves to devoting a clearly specified amount of time to the mentoring relationship and honor those commitments

- the mentors give to their mentees the benefit of their full and unedited experience, warts and all.

We recommend that at an early meeting, mentor and mentee discuss and agree their respective roles in the relationship. The mentor may ask the mentee for a summary of her ambitions and goals, for example, or barriers she sees to her success; her priorities; and the criteria by which she will judge the success of the mentoring afterwards. These judgments are provisional. They may change during the mentoring. The mentor might not agree with them, and may try to persuade his mentee to adopt different goals or priorities.

As part of the contracting process, the parties agree how often they will meet, who is responsible for setting up meetings, at what point they will review the effectiveness of the relationship and so on. We are also involved at this setup stage, helping mentor and mentee to reach agreement on the ground rules of their relationship.

Confidentiality and trust are the foundations of any relationship of this kind, and a willingness to listen and empathize is its driving force. It is a strange type of meeting for mentors, because they are not expected to solve problems, or provide any answers. They must be willing to challenge mentees strongly, but tactfully; give feedback when appropriate; and act as sounding boards on private and personal matters, when necessary. Above all, they must encourage their mentees to become the authors of their own destinies and to find the courage and confidence to realize their potential.

The essence of mentoring is conversation. As the senior partner, the mentor takes the initiative in the early stages. As the relationship develops, the two personal narratives merge and the project, which is the realization of the mentee's ambition, becomes a joint venture in which both parties have investment.

Achievements

Irene Dorner became a mentee on the FTSE 100 Cross-Company Mentoring Programme in early 2005, while serving as general manager northern division at HSBC, the UK's largest banking group. In 2007, she was appointed deputy chairman and CEO of HSBC Malaysia and group general manager of HSBC Group.

Shortly before leaving London to take up her new job, Irene spoke to one of the authors about her mentoring experience. She believed that the contact she had had with her mentor, Paul Skinner, chairman of Rio Tinto plc, had been instrumental in her success. She said she'd enjoyed her meetings with him and felt the opportunity the program provided to talk offline with someone outside her own organization had been extremely valuable. She'd used him as a sounding board, and a wise and experienced counsellor. She mentioned a particular internal issue she had discussed with him in depth (she didn't go into details), and said the whole program would have been worth it for the one piece of advice her mentor gave her on that issue.

Although we cannot prove a causal connection, the careers of many of the program's mentees have developed significantly during or after their mentoring. Six have been appointed to the executive committees of their own companies as group executive directors; and two of them now sit on their companies' main boards. Several have been promoted to important international positions. One mentee has taken a lateral move from a functional role to global operations director, thereby gaining more relevant experience for a board position. One has been appointed a NED of the UK's University for Industry, another is now CEO of an independent media group, a third has been appointed to the regional board of a national charity, a fourth has been appointed to the board of the Department of Work and Pensions, and a fifth to the board of an NHS Trust. All of these are major career achievements of course, but most gratifying for us, in view of the program's formal objectives, is that three mentees have been appointed as NEDs to the boards of major UK companies.

The program's spring 2007 update reported Irene Dorner's overseas appointment referred to above, and the appointment of another of our mentees, Anne Bouverot, as the director of international development at France Télécom, a member of the Conseil Scientifique, and chairman of France Télécom, New York.

During 2007, we worked with the European Professional Women's Network (EPWN) and Diafora on a program based on, and informed by, the FTSE 100 Cross-Company Mentoring Programme model, but adapted to suit the French market. At a breakfast meeting in Paris hosted by Dr. Bertrand Collomb, président d'honneur of Lafarge, the leaders of six companies in the CAC 40 and large public enterprises met to discuss the creation of a cross-company mentoring initiative based on the UK program. They resolved to establish BoardWomen Partners to:

1. *Identifier et préparer un vivier de femmes en collaboration avec leurs employeurs.*

   (Identify and prepare a pool of women who can be ready to become non-executive directors, in coordination with their companies.)

2. *Donner à ces femmes une meilleure visibilité, afin qu'elles puissent être connues et repérées par les comités de nomination.*

   (Provide these women with more visibility outside their company, so that they are known to nomination committees.)

3. *Les mettre en contact directement avec les PDG ou les Présidents des conseils d'administration à travers un programme de mentoring et de mise en réseau inter-entreprises.*

(Put them in contact with executive chairmen ('PDG') or non-executive chairmen through a cross-company mentoring and networking program.)

Six months after the initial meeting, Diafora and EPWN were confident that French business leaders might support a non-profit program to promote gender diversity on non-executive boards, but felt that they would be less willing to mentor than their UK counterparts, because mentoring was a less familiar concept in French business. So Diafora and EPWN, supported by Praesta, are taking time to adapt the French program to the needs of French business leaders and to incorporate certain program additions they have suggested, such as encouraging the appointments of women at CAC 40 companies to the boards of group subsidiaries, as a stepping-stone to a corporate board position.

BoardWomen Partners hasn't until now disclosed information about the program because, as a président-directeur général explained: "we will communicate when we have tangible successes." However, with a core team of six founder presidents and CEOs from CAC 40 companies and contacts already established with some 50 presidents and CEOs of large companies and public enterprises, the organizers are confident that BoardWomen Partners is well placed to make a major contribution to gender diversity at board level in CAC 40 companies and public enterprises in France.

In addition to supporting the French program, we were delighted to be consulted by Thea Miller, of Patrick O'Callaghan & Associates, founding sponsors of Women on Board™ Mentoring Program, which was launched in Canada in May, 2007. A leading article, headlined "Breaking the board-room barrier," on the launch in the *Globe and Mail*, Canada's newspaper of record, mentioned the UK program as an inspiration. Other sponsors of the Canadian program are the Richard Ivey School of Business, the Canadian Institute of Chartered Accountants, CN and Korn/Ferry International. Seven companies had agreed to participate. Patrick O'Callaghan, chair of Women on Board, said:

> There has been a lot of talk over the years about the lack of gender diversity on corporate boards, but very little has actually been done about it. In its own small way this program is being proactive in addressing this issue, by showing that leading Canadian companies are concerned about board gender diversity and by developing a cadre of women director candidates that have been mentored by some of Canada's most influential business leaders.

At the time of writing (January, 2008), we were also in contact with companies in three other countries about launching similar programs.

Program development

Here in the UK, we're receiving overwhelmingly positive feedback from mentees about the support, challenges and insights they are getting from mentors. But we're not resting on our laurels. The program is under continual development, because we are constantly learning more about the challenges faced by women who want to be appointed to FTSE 100 boards and how best to address them.

We have created a small strategy and consultation unit with a few of the chairmen to see whether it may be possible to make progress more quickly in some situations with targeted, personal interventions. We have formed strategic alliances with some executive search firms who are interested in the program and understand the issues. In response to feedback from mentors, headhunters and some mentees about the value of the program's development opportunities, we have divided the mentees into groups, according to their perceived readiness for NED appointments, and tailored each group's development accordingly.

We see this book as part of the program's development too, because it's designed to crystallize, in an accessible form, much of what we have learned from our mentors and mentees over the past three years. As we explained in the introduction, the book is based on what we've christened the "roadmap"; a simple matrix that outlines the various steps senior female executives need to take, if they want to improve their chances of being appointed a NED or an executive director and how to take them. The roadmap is shown in Table 1.2.

The challenge summarized

An early version of what became the roadmap appeared in *The Times* in May 2007,[13] in a list we gave to Penny Wark for her article on why so few ambitious women were being appointed to UK boards. We will be working through the roadmap in the chapters that follow and will add, in the sections at the end of the prescriptive chapters (2–9), some reflections on the implications for companies and company-like organizations of the chapter's main points. We end this chapter with a summary of the roadmap's key components.

TABLE 1.2

WHAT? (the eight challenges) / HOW? (process)	DECIDING TO ENGAGE Take the decision; build understanding of milieu; get to grips with politics *Chapter 2*	THE WRITTEN RULES OF ENGAGEMENT Build understanding of board basics: corporate governance, NED role, board and committee structure, board finance *Chapter 3*	THE UNWRITTEN RULES Build understanding of board dynamics and social etiquette *Chapter 4*
Keeping up to date via reading: • Cadbury, Hempel, Higgs, Tyson Reports • Combined Code, Female FTSE Report • *A Woman's Place is in the Boardroom* • Corporate governance booklist	X	X	
Learning from mentors and the FTSE 100 Cross-Company Mentoring Programme	X	X	X
Maintaining contact with search consultants (including development programs run by them)		X	
Learning from a coach	X	X	X
Attending training and development programs	X	X	
Learning from existing women directors	X	X	X
Learning from personal presence consultants			
Being on other boards e.g. charitable, public sector, FTSE 350, private equity		X	X
Networking			
Changing job roles and taking internal board positions			X
Speaking at conferences or for industry groups; writing articles			

A SENSE OF DIRECTION	CULTIVATING BOARD QUALITIES	SETTING OUT YOUR STALL	MIND THE GAP	BOARD GAMES
Identify sectors and companies which are of interest. Do homework: look at the boards and the people on them	Develop awareness, visibility, profile, image and presence	Produce "personal marketing plan" based on grasp of own selling points; personal appetite; how to contribute	Identify areas of personal learning from feedback. Engage in behavioral change if necessary. Authentic leadership	Build experience for top boards: break onto first board; gain operational experience
Chapter 5	Chapter 6	Chapter 7	Chapter 8	Chapter 9
X				
X	X	X	X	
X	X	X		
X	X	X	X	
			X	
	X	X	X	
	X			
	X			X
X	X			
	X			X
X	X			

Deciding to engage

Do you like the idea of being a main board director? If you're reading this book, your answer is probably yes. What's not to like, for an able and successful executive, about becoming a member of the elite group who govern our commercial and industrial life? You may like the idea in principle, but do you really, seriously aspire to the board? Have you imagined what it would be like, confronted all the consequences and legal responsibilities, weighed up the pros and cons, and made a well-informed and robust decision?

The written rules of engagement

A decision to engage in the board game will be an emotional, as well as an intellectual one in most cases, but it should be based on as dispassionate an assessment as possible of your own intellectual and psychological suitability for the job, and a thorough investigation of what becoming a director will entail. Much of this book will help you to assess yourself. We devote this short chapter to helping you address the easier task of getting up to speed with the formal legal status and responsibilities of boards and their directors within the modern corporate governance system.

The unwritten rules

Laws, regulations and codes of practice are the framework within which boards operate. Board candidates must also understand the unwritten rules, conventions and traditions. They vary, of course, from company to company, but some are common to all and all are common to some.

A sense of direction

It is not enough to want to be on a board, any board. Women aspiring to board-level positions should identify the industries and types of organization that interest them and particular organizations within them where the chances of board or equivalent appointments for women seem relatively high.

Cultivating board qualities

Even the most coherent and authentic personalities will have various different personae that they assume for different environments. Women who aspire to board positions need to choose their most suitable persona for the board and develop, refine and promote that persona. This is likely to involve some kind of personal rapprochement with the macho culture that still dominates the board environment or "milieu" as we call it.

Setting out your stall

Men tend to think more systematically about their careers than women and develop clearer maps of their career paths. Women are inclined to let their careers happen and, as a consequence, often get stuck in the traditional female areas, such as HR and marketing (so-called "pink collar" functions), that rarely lead to the board. They should draft personal marketing plans and try to spend time in parts of the business that have proven in the past to produce board members.

Mind the gap

Plans are necessary, but they are not sufficient. Women also need to appear to have the leadership qualities to be appointed to a board. They must achieve self-awareness and identify gaps and weaknesses in their styles and ways of handling others, and change their styles if necessary, while remaining authentic and impressive personalities.

Board games

The best preparation for a main board and among the best credentials when applying for main board positions is service as a non-executive director of a subsidiary or some other organization, such as a small non-competing company, or charity, and senior roles, such as being a member of the executive committee, at your own company.

The map is not the territory

These are the key challenges for women with board ambitions. They've been validated by our chairmen mentors in the FTSE 100 Cross-Company Mentoring Programme and have proved very helpful to our mentees. But it's one thing to have a helpful roadmap and quite another to arrive at your destination within a reasonable amount of time and with your self-respect intact.

In the following chapters, we will look more closely at each of these aspects of the challenge faced by women with board ambitions and try to give an impression of the kinds of territories they will be passing through.

References

1. *2006 Catalyst Census of Women Board Directors of the Fortune 500*, Catalyst, 2007.
2. *The Female FTSE Report 2006: Identifying the New Generation of Women Directors*, Cranfield University School of Management, 2006.
3. *The Gender Agenda*, Equal Opportunities Commission, 2007.
4. *The Female FTSE Report 2007: A Year of Encouraging Progress*, Cranfield University School of Management, 2007.
5. *Catalyst Census of Women Board Directors, Corporate Officers, and Top Earners of the Fortune 500*, Catalyst, December 2007.
6. *Off-Ramps and On-Ramps: Keeping Talented Women on the Road to Success*, Sylvia Ann Hewlett, Harvard Business School Press, 2007.
7. www.managers.org.uk.
8. *The Bottom Line: Connecting Corporate Performance and Gender Diversity*, Catalyst, sponsored by BMO Financial Group, 2004.
9. *The Bottom Line: Corporate Performance and Women's Representation on Boards*, Catalyst, sponsored by The Chubb Corporation, 2007.
10. *Women Matter: Gender Diversity, a Corporate Performance Driver*, McKinsey & Company, 2007.
11. "Luxottica eyes top jobs for women," *Financial Times*, December 4, 2007.
12. "Mentors to help women onto boards," Alison Maitland, *Financial Times,* October 21, 2004.
13. "With prejudice," Penny Wark, *Times2*, May 22, 2007.

CHAPTER 2

Deciding to engage

If you're tempted by this, why would you say no? If you've got this far, why would you not *go for it?*

Sir Philip Hampton, chairman, J Sainsbury plc

It begins with curiosity – What would it be like to be a main board director? Am I good enough? If the traffic lights stay green as you move up the hierarchy, your curiosity makes you alert for the weak signals the less curious would miss; that the powers that be in and around your organization see you as a star and, by implication, a potential main board member. Your "why?" becomes "why not?" Your self-confidence grows. You begin to believe that you are good enough and no insuperable obstacles bar the way. Belief becomes a wish and the wish becomes an intent.

It may be years before the right opportunity arises, but you have to be prepared, emotionally, when it does arrive. You must have weighed the pros and cons, and decided that the former outweigh the latter. Luck will play a part of course, but if your mind isn't prepared, you may not see the opportunity when it arises, or, if you do, you may not react quickly or effectively enough.

A perceived asymmetry between men and women here is illustrated by a pair of dead poets. Shakespeare said in *Julius Caesar*:[1]

> There is a tide in the affairs of men,
> Which, taken at the flood, leads on to fortune;

In his parody of the bard, Lord Byron suggested that, although tides were gender neutral, fortune was a male thing:[2]

> There is a tide in the affairs of women,
> Which, taken at the flood, leads – God knows where.

Women must ready themselves for the flood tide more deliberately than men. For able and ambitious men there's no "why?" They don't have to think about it. As we argued in our first book, they are programed by their nature to strive for the top. Unlike women, men are natural hierarchy climbers. It may take a deliberate and painful act of will for an able and hitherto successful man to withdraw voluntarily from the competition for leadership positions.

It's the other way around for most women. For them an act of will is required to throw their hats into the ring.

HATS IN THE RING !

© Barbara Shore

Alertness and decisiveness

Men don't have to decide to watch out for weak signals, because this also comes naturally to the natural hierarchy climber. Alertness for weak signals is an integral part of a hierarchy climber's equipment.

A colleague of ours was a bank manager. Because she was one of very few female managers at that time, she was invited to the chairman's dinner. "At least I knew I had to accept," she recalled. She sat next to an area director – a senior manager at her boss's level. They got on very well. Towards the end of the meal, he asked her if she'd ever thought of moving to an area director's office. "I didn't realize it was a job offer," she said wistfully, "so I said, 'I don't think so. I love having my own branch.'" He said, "OK, that's interesting." "Some other woman got the job," she reflected ruefully. "It would have been great for me. I would have stayed there a year and then got another promotion. He saw the dinner as an opportunity to get to know me. He could have handled it differently, but by not expressing interest, I effectively withdrew. A man would have known. Women don't go looking. I believed that, if someone wanted to hire me, he or she would approach me directly. Our values and beliefs box us in."

But it is not enough to be alert. If hierarchy climbing doesn't come naturally to you, you must also be consciously decisive. When a door opens for an ambitious and alert woman, a decision must often be made very quickly, before it closes. Many factors must be considered and many anxieties must be confronted. Is this the right opportunity? Will I regret it if I don't go for it? (The bank manager did.) Am I good enough? Could I contribute and make a difference? What will I have to sacrifice? Do I want the legal responsibilities? (More on that in the next chapter.) Will I be able to cope with the pressure and play the politics effectively?

In some cases, whether or not the pros outweigh the cons could depend partly on economic factors. Time is money after all. A woman already juggling a full-time management role with domestic responsibilities may be unable to afford, or unwilling to give, her time away as a NED for the proverbial pittance. NED fees vary enormously, depending on the size of the company, among other things, but a 2006 survey by Incomes Data Services (IDS) of FTSE 350 companies found that fees to NEDs averaged £40,000 per year, excluding payments for serving on board committees. This was 13 percent more than in 2005, reflecting, according to IDS, the wider scope of the NED role and the consequent reduction in the number of qualified people available.[3]

Some of the factors you will have to consider when an opportunity is presented to you will be specific to that opportunity, but many will be general and can and should be addressed before an opportunity has presented itself.

Unlike men, you can't rely on your natural instincts to compel you to grab opportunities when they present themselves. You must condition yourself to react quickly and positively to opportunities, by going through the pros and the cons beforehand, imagining what it would be like to be on a board and how your personality, style, aptitudes and skills will play there. An essential part of this preparation is the development of a general understanding of the nature of what we call the "boardspace." If you aspire to be on a board, you'd better have a pretty good idea of what kind of place it is or, rather, what kind of space it is.

We will look at some of the formal, legal features of the boardspace in the next chapter, but you'll need to understand something of its general nature before you can decide whether it's a space you really want to enter.

Boardspace

One of the most important features of a board that a board candidate needs to understand is that, although people (including ourselves in the titles of our books) talk of getting into the boardroom, being a director is more than having access to a particular room, to which non-directors are denied entry.

For newly appointed directors, as Monica Burch, partner and member of the board of law firm, Addleshaw Goddard LLP, puts it: "the board is a different space for the new woman director, but it's not a *place*." Board-level activities and conversations are not confined to the boardroom. The boardroom is the place where important decisions are made, but it's not generally the place where minds are made up, arguments are put forward, or debates are conducted. The board meeting has a special legal status, but it's usually the formal culmination of a series of decision-making events, not the event itself.

"The conversations in the margins of a board meeting are vital," says Monica. "They set the scenes and oil the tongues." Pre-presentations and corridor work, water-cooler chats, canvassing, lobbying – boards couldn't operate without these. Directors are a special group of men and women, with some clearly defined legal responsibilities, as well as some not so clearly defined social and ethical responsibilities. They're directors all the time, not once a month. Their conversation is continuous, not periodic.

An appointment to a board of a listed company, as opposed to that of the subsidiary of a listed company or a private company, brings you to the interfaces between the organization and its environments. The board isn't just customer facing; it's also investor facing, capital markets facing, law facing, regulator facing, local community facing and general public facing. The directors are the personifications of the company. All the bucks stop with them.

One of the mentors on the FTSE 100 Cross-Company Mentoring Programme advises board candidates to

> stop and consider what actually goes on on a board. You are working alongside people who you may only see at eight board meetings a year and perhaps a board strategy awayday and then any work you put in on a Nomco [nomination committee] or Remco [remuneration committee]. The pressures on directors, including non-executive directors, are now so acute that no board member can fail to be conscious that the board as a group is sharing responsibility for a considerable amount of risk. That makes it essential to build trust between board members; because you're in the group *as* a group; sharing the risks and responsibility for the strategic leadership of the company.

Board work is riddled with conflicts of interests, conflicts of duty and conflicts between interests and duties. Directors have a duty to the shareholders who appoint them to maximize shareholder value, and a responsibility, under the law, to ensure that the company's search for value is conducted lawfully. Their interests in preserving their own reputations tend to make them risk averse, particularly if they are NEDs, and yet they also have a duty to their investors to take, or approve the taking of, commercial risks. They are the official formulators of the company's strategy and the guardians of its conscience and its reputation. They have a natural loyalty to their co-directors, but a duty collectively to ensure that the company complies with the laws and regulations relating to tax, health and safety, the environment, equal opportunities, bribery, financial and other kinds of reporting, and so on.

Directors deal with issues that are not as clear as those with which they dealt below board level. A strategy, plan or project for which there is clearly a strong business case can't be nodded through at board level. Other factors in addition to the commercial merits must be taken into account. Board-space is social and ethical, as well as commercial. It may not be where the power lies, that's usually in the executive committee, but it's where the use of power is governed and, if necessary, restrained.

This intimacy with power makes the boardspace, including the spaces where new board members are selected, inherently political. There is no getting away from this. People who apply for board positions must accept that they aspire to a political office, that they must engage in politics and that politics will inevitably play an important part in determining whether or not their applications are successful.

Most women dislike corporate politics and try to keep well away from it – they are more reluctant than most men to play political games and they don't think they're very good at them. Their distaste stems partly from a common failure to understand what politics is and does (why it is both inevitable and necessary; see below), partly from an often justified suspicion that there is so much of it that it leads to injustice and inefficiency and distracts male colleagues from the task of creating value for their shareholders (or their equivalents) and partly, it seems to us anyway, from a curious difference in the meanings that men and women attach to the words often associated with the term "corporate politics."

Playing games

A comment from two female (but no male) readers of earlier drafts of this book was that "playing politics" didn't seem quite right and we should use another term, such as "working the politics" or "engaging in politics" instead. For women, it seems, playing is something children do, and when you become a woman, you put away such childish things. Women see game playing as a frivolous (or, more literally, a ludicrous) pastime for adults. They know that men play games, but they describe them with the pejorative term "playboy" when they do.

Men don't see play in the same way. In addition to being something children do, playing, or rather playing well, is making the best possible legal (within the rules) moves in the current circumstances of the game. (And by the way, when a father plays a board game (forgive the pun) with his son, he tries to win not, although it may seem that way to his wife, because he gets pleasure from winning, even against his five-year-old son, but because he must teach his son that there's no point in playing games unless both sides are trying to win.)

There is nothing fundamentally frivolous or ludicrous about playing a game for men. Men see games everywhere; in love, work and war, as well as in sport and politics. Child's play is preparation for adult play, not something you put away when you become a man. Game playing is a serious business. An entire branch of mathematics, game theory, is devoted to it, and has led to important insights in areas ranging from military strategy and evolution theory, to business competition and international relations.

This is the meaning the reader should attribute to any references to game playing. When we write about playing politics in this chapter and elsewhere in this book, we don't mean playing *at* politics. We mean playing the game of politics – making the best possible legal (within the written and unwritten rules) moves available to you, the player, in the current circumstances of the game.

If the board is your destination, you cannot avoid politics. You must understand, and take an interest in, how your organization, and how organizations in general, work. You can do this in your own way. You are not obliged to play politics in the same way men do, but play it you must, in one way or another. If you decide to go for it, you must accept both the inevitability and the necessity of politics and come to terms with your need to be part of it; to be a player.

Men don't have to decide deliberately to engage in politics, because this also comes naturally to a natural hierarchy climber. Politics, and the social networking associated with it, is an essential part of a hierarchy climber's skill set. Most men do it without thinking. For a man, to be an ambitious animal is to be a political animal.

The inevitability of politics

Company politics has had a bad press. Although we accept politics as both natural and necessary in a democracy – too little is worse than too much, because political activity shows that democracy is working and the market for power is open – corporate politics is abhorred by many men, as well as most women. Why is this? Why is a quality we regard as healthy in social governance so often seen as contemptible in corporate governance?

THE INEVITABILITY OF POLITICS . . .

© Barbara Shore

Politicians seeking to gain or retain power are active in all social groups. In a democracy, competition for power is open and regulated by well-understood rules. But in companies, the competition is secret and largely unregulated. We all know it goes on, but many of us see it as an inevitable, but unnecessary evil, the less talked about the better. We abhor it, because we suspect (particularly if we believe that others are better than we are at playing politics) that it produces unjust outcomes, and it reeks of patronage and conspiracy. Moreover, messy, public rows can tarnish a company's reputation and damage its stock rating.

But power holds organizations together and some process is needed to assign it. In politics, as in many other areas, the poison is in the dose. There can be too much politics in business, within and between companies, but power has to be assigned in one way or another.

Power can be assigned according to competence or influence. They are the only two possible criteria, because a process of assigning power that involves neither defaults to time served and few people believe that is a recipe for success in business.

A pure meritocracy is the ideal most people espouse, but it is far from being the fair, clear system it is made out to be. How is merit established? If through polls or peer reviews, how can we be sure such processes are untainted by undercover politics, and what if the most competent person is widely disliked, or lacks the social skills to use the power she or he has been assigned?

Power assignment processes based purely on influence can lead to the worst kind of cronyism, but processes based entirely on competence can lead to an atmosphere of hostility and to a lack of cooperation that can be just as bad. Competence and influence are both necessary criteria in the assignment of power, but neither is sufficient.

However competent people are, they will not become effective leaders unless they are connected to the networks of influence that make the organization steerable. Outlawing the trade in influence, and patron and protégé relationships, would undermine the corporate governance process by denying it an essential lubricant.

The dangers of a rigorously meritocratic system, in which merit is defined purely in terms of competence, are that the company may end up with people in top positions whom no one likes, supports or trusts and from whom decisions that work in practice (as opposed to those that are right in theory) cannot, therefore, be expected.

The personal mentoring of protégés is, and always has been, a feature of all dynamic societies and institutions, because it's the best way so far devised to develop leaders who have enough influence to carry their organizations with them.

Effective leaders often achieve their positions through the advocacy of mentors. It is true that this can lead to clone successors, but it can also produce radical leaders, willing and empowered by their extensive influence networks (including those inherited from their sponsors, as well as those they create themselves) to take a company in a new direction.

Assignments of power in organizations must be objective, in terms of competence, and subjective, in terms of influence, because without influence, competence is powerless. Those who refrain from so-called "politicking," because they find it distasteful or lack the aptitude for it, are effectively withdrawing themselves as serious candidates for high corporate office.

Getting to grips with politics

Once you have grasped the nettle and accepted that, whether you like it or not, you must engage in politics, you should give some thought to the way you're going to play it.

The difficulty for women here is that the political game's unwritten rules have, so far at any rate, been unwritten by men. Until women unwrite another set of rules that suit women, they will find it hard to play the game effectively without appearing to be unfeminine and thus lacking authenticity. This is a difficult problem to which there is no easy solution. Each woman must find her own way to play the political game effectively, without denying her nature and being "uncomfortable in her own skin," as one of our mentees put it.

We will delve further into corporate politics and how women can play the game effectively in Chapter 4. Our purpose in bringing the issue up here is to emphasize that coming to terms with the inevitability and necessity of politics is a necessary, preliminary emotional step before you can decide to play the board game.

Reflections for companies

There's not a lot an individual company can do to make it easier for women to decide to engage. Such decisions are based on many factors, only a few of which are within one company's control. And they are usually made long before the woman achieves a position that's within reach of the board.

At the margin, however, a company that openly expresses eagerness to appoint women to its board could tip the balance for some women, and will certainly make itself a significantly more attractive employer to ambitious women. A company in which women occupy senior positions or even board positions makes that "why?" question a female employee asks herself, when deciding whether or not to engage, more likely to be replaced by "why not?"

Women look sideways as well as upwards when contemplating their next moves and their ultimate aims. If they see other women moving up the hierarchy alongside them, they will feel more comfortable.

It is hard to exaggerate the emotional strain of being in a place in which you're marked by your gender as a lone alien. Nancy Astor, the first woman to take her seat in the House of Commons as Conservative MP for Plymouth South in 1919, illustrated this when interviewed on the BBC's *Woman's Hour* by Mary Stocks – later Baroness Stocks – in 1956.

"Was it a relief," Stocks enquired at one point, "when Mrs Wintringham [the second woman elected MP, for the Liberals in 1921] came to join you?" Nancy Astor replied:

> Oh yes, she was perfectly wonderful. I mean she couldn't have been nicer, but do you know, it's a funny thing, she could never sit in that House unless I was there. She said to me afterwards she couldn't do it. The atmosphere of not being wanted is not very easy, is it?

It wasn't just in their minds, either. Later in the interview, Astor recalled another revealing incident:

> Even my best friends couldn't speak to me, they really couldn't, not in the House … I met him [Winston Churchill] at dinner about two years afterwards [after she took her seat]. He said to me, "It's a very remarkable performance." I said, "What?" He said, "You staying where you are." And I said, "Well, Winston, why on earth didn't you speak to me?" He said, "We hoped to freeze you out," and he added, "When you entered the House of Commons I felt as if a woman had entered my bathroom and I'd nothing to protect myself with, except a sponge." I asked him, "Did it never occur to you that your appalling appearance might have been protection enough?"[4]

One would hope that it's easier for women MPs now and certainly male MPs shouldn't need sponges to protect themselves any more. That's because the style of politics has been changed by female MPs. Men and women have got more used to each other in the House of Commons. Together they are developing a way to play the game of politics that works for both genders.

The same thing will happen in corporate politics. Boards have a long way to go to match the gender balance in the House of Commons (about 20 percent women, at the time of writing), but a smart company will realize that the style of its politics must change to accommodate women, and will try to eliminate questionable aspects of its power assignment system and the overtly and covertly macho aspects of its internal politics. A competitive advantage in the war for talent could be gained by a system that rewards, with assignments of more power, those employing the more diplomatic, female style of politics.

The power of three

Research reported in the *Harvard Business Review* in December 2006 found that lone women on boards often feel isolated, like Mrs Wintringham. The appointment of a second woman helps to solve the isolation problem, but can also create new problems if men suspect a female conspiracy. Alison Konrad and Vicki Kramer interviewed 50 female directors, 12 CEOs and 7 company secretaries at Fortune 1000 companies. They found that a clear shift occurs when there are three or more women on a board. At that stage, the women directors cease to be novelties to which incumbent male directors feel the need to adapt, and become merely directors. Boardroom dynamics change, allowing the hitherto latent synergies of gender balance to emerge.[5]

The result is strikingly consistent with the Catalyst and McKinsey gender and performance studies we quoted in the previous chapter and to a somewhat lesser extent with the results of another recent study by Cranfield School of Management, which found less stereotyping, a broader perspective and a friendlier atmosphere, if there are two or more women on the board.[6]

Together these studies show that tokenism doesn't work. Two women on the board is better for women (queen bees excepted) than one, and better for boards and corporate performance, too. And three seems to be better than two.

But enough of these betters! What business wants to know is what's best. If three's better than two, is four better than three and five better than four? If the question is about main boards and corporate performance, the answer is: we don't know. There are not enough data on which to base firm conclusions. Most large companies have at least one woman on their boards now, about a third have more than one, but few have more than two. We can compare the performance of firms with none, one, two and, at a pinch, three women on the board, but that's as far as it goes.

An interesting hint about what we might find if we did have the data to study the company performance effects of the whole gender balance range, from all men to all women, is provided by the results of new research by Professor Lynda Gratton and her team at London Business School. They studied the innovation performance of over 100 teams in 17 countries, including the full range of gender mixes. They focused on four variables known to be important stimuli for innovation:

■ the "psychological safety" of the whole team and its members

■ the self-confidence of the team and its members

■ the extent to which they are prepared to take risks and experiment

■ the general efficiency of the team.

Gratton and her team reported:

> We found that for all these critical factors, the optimal gender mix was about 50% men and 50% women. We also found that a slight majority of women creates optimal conditions in relation to the self confidence of the team.[7]

As we saw in Chapter 1, the Italian sunglasses group Luxottica takes the same view about gender diversity and innovation.

Politics self-test

If there's one thing that puts women off taking the emotional plunge and deciding to play the board game, it's politics. It comes up time and again in our day jobs working with senior women, and in the FTSE 100 Cross-Company Mentoring Programme. "I like the idea of being on a board, but I worry about whether I can handle the politics." "I've been approached to join a board, but it's a snake pit." "Ethics and social responsibility are important values for me – I'm not the sort of person who can sacrifice friendships to get on."

As we have suggested, such misgivings are partly based on a mistaken but common perception of corporate politics. To help you get an idea of where you stand currently on corporate politics and the direction in which you need to move, locate yourself on the grid shown in Figure 2.1. The matrix has been adapted from a paper by Simon Baddeley and Kim James at the University of Birmingham, entitled "Owl, fox, donkey or sheep: political skills for managers."[8] Although it is 20 years old now, we have found this model resonates strongly with most women on this topic in women's leadership development programs, wherever in the world they are run.

Figure 2.1 locates an individual's general attitude and approach to corporate politics according to the depth of understanding of how an organization in general, and his or her organization in particular, works, and the degree to which the individual behaves politically in his or her own interests, or in the interests of the organization as a whole.

The *inept* box (self-interested, low organizational understanding) is a mostly male preserve, inhabited by those who rush in where angels fear to tread. They are often politically active, but, because they don't know the rules, they make mistakes and fools of themselves and don't get very far.

The ones who realize they're going nowhere, because they're shooting in the dark, and take some trouble to learn those unwritten rules of the political game, move up into the *clever* box. They continue to be in it for what they can get out of it, and keep trying to manipulate the system for their own ends, but make more progress, because their moves are better informed and they are quicker on their feet. Some women think being clever in this sense is the essence of corporate politics, which is why they find it so distasteful.

There are a lot of women in the *naïve* box. They are well meaning and always act in good faith, but because they're innocent, ignorant and risk averse, they are seldom active politically. This is the default box for those who don't like politics.

The objective, of course, is to move from wherever you think you are towards the *wise* box. The owls understand the rules of the game and how their organization works, but they have high integrity and, when playing the political game, they are motivated by the organization's as well as their own interests. They're active politically, can be assertive when necessary, but they're always open and honest.

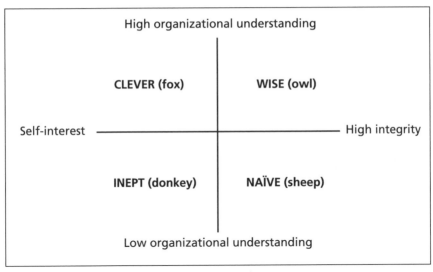

Figure 2.1 Personal politics locator

So the challenge here is to derive from your values and beliefs, and from your understanding of the organization, a wise (as opposed to a clever or a naïve) way of playing the political game.

How wise are you? Is there anyone in your organization who seems, to you, to be playing the game wisely? If so, watch and learn.

References

1. *Julius Caesar*, Act IV, Scene 3.
2. *Don Juan*, Canto VI, st. 2.
3. *Executive Compensation Review*, Incomes Data Services, 2006.
4. *Woman's Hour: from Joyce Grenfell to Sharon Osbourne: Celebrating Sixty Years of Women's Lives*, various authors, BBC, 2006, also available in hardback.
5. "How many women do boards need?" *Harvard Business Review*, December 2006.
6. *The Female FTSE Report*, Cranfield University School of Management, 2006.
7. *Innovative Potential: Men and Women in Teams*, The Lehman Brothers Centre for Women in Business, London Business School, 2007.
8. "Owl, fox, donkey or sheep: political skills for managers," Simon Baddeley and Kim James, *Management Education and Development*, **18**(1), 1987, pp. 3–19.

CHAPTER 3

The written rules of engagement

Good corporate governance has a ring of abstract formality, but it has the potential to add real business value and reduce business risk. It's about ensuring clarity and accountability in key roles.

Paul Skinner, chairman, Rio Tinto plc

It is one thing to accept that boards are political arenas and quite another to understand the kind of political arena, and the contexts in which it operates, that you will enter when you're appointed to a board. Company politics may not be governed or regulated in the same way as national politics, but the role of the director is defined by and subject to a complex framework of laws, regulations and codes of practice. Managers who aspire to be directors must realize that this means there is a huge difference between being a manager and being a director. They must study and understand that difference. If company politics is informal, in the sense that it operates without written rules, corporate governance – in the form of laws, regulations and codes of practice – is its formal counterpart.

Governance history

The origins of modern corporate governance date back to a major flaw in the original design of the joint stock company identified by Adam Smith after the Bubble Act of 1720 had given it limited liability. His criticism of the joint stock company with limited liability was that, because its directors were "managers ... of other people's money," they couldn't be expected to "watch over it with the same anxious vigilance with which the partners in a private copartnery [partnership] frequently watch over their own."[1]

The trade of a joint stock company was managed by directors, subject to the control of a general court of proprietors (the modern general meeting). Smith observed, scathingly:

> But the greater part of those proprietors [shareholders] seldom pretend to understand anything of the business of the company; and ... give themselves no trouble about it, but receive contentedly such ... dividends as the directors think proper to make them. This total exemption from trouble and from risk beyond a limited

sum encourages many people to become adventurers in joint stock companies, who would on no account hazard their fortunes in any private copartnery.
Such companies, therefore, commonly draw to themselves much greater stocks
[capital, in modern parlance] than any private copartnery can boast of.

This was the problem – enormous sums committed by ignorant investors
exempted "from trouble and from risk beyond a limited sum" into the care
of directors not motivated by ownership to watch over it with "the same
anxious vigilance" of true partners. (An aspiring director should be aware,
however, that although UK investors remain exempted "from risk beyond a
limited sum," statutory directors have unlimited liability.)

Smith's critique was voiced again in 1933 by Adolf Berle and Gardiner
Means, after the limited liability, joint stock company had become the domi-
nant business institution. They observed that in most of America's largest
companies control had passed to management.[2] As Berle said later, in 1959:

> stockholders, though still politely called "owners", are passive. They have the
> right to receive [on condition] … that they do not interfere in management.
> Neither in law nor, as a rule, in fact do they have that capacity.[3]

This separation of ownership and control in limited liability, joint stock
companies gave rise to the notion of agency costs; the costs that those in
control (the directors) impose on those who own (the shareholders) when,
as the paid agents of owners, they act in their own, rather than their princi-
pals', interests. Directors impose costs on shareholders, for instance, when
they are incompetent, corrupt or (because they know there is strong correlation between the size of a company and the size of its leaders' pay packets)
they pursue growth at the expense of shareholder returns.

Some control over agency costs imposed on shareholders by delinquent
executives is provided by the takeover system and by modern activist fund
managers who do understand the companies they invest in and are very far
from being the compliant shareholders Adam Smith described. But they are
blunt forms of control that are usually exercised after private shareholders
have incurred significant costs.

The separation of ownership and control and the agency costs that it can,
and often does, give rise to are the origins and inspiration of the modern
panoply of laws, regulations, rules and codes of practice that has come to be
known, collectively, as "corporate governance." In theory and also in law, a
company's directors are the servants of its shareholders, but, like medieval
barons, they're overmighty subjects who must be controlled.

It is not only investors who have demanded and obtained, through the legislature and the courts, protection from the possibility that the directors of the companies they own may abuse their power. Companies have always been subject to the laws of the land, of course, in such areas as terms and conditions of employment, health and safety, tax and environmental protection. But after a crop of corporate scandals in recent years (Enron, World-Com, Parmalat, Maxwell), governments all over the world have taken deliberate and, in some cases, draconian steps (for example the Sarbanes-Oxley Act in the US) to reduce the freedom of company boards to govern themselves and to deploy as they see fit the enormous economic power on the balance sheets and in the pension funds of global corporations.

Enough has been published about corporate governance and the role of directors in recent years to account for a small rain forest. We are not equipped nor inclined to add materially to the literature here, but a brief survey of the subject plus a few suggestions for further reading may be helpful.

Modern corporate governance

The components of the corporate governance system include:

- laws, such as the UK Companies Act 2006, European Union (EU) Directives and the Sarbanes-Oxley Act in the US

- regulations promulgated and policed by institutions such as the UK's Financial Services Authority (FSA) and the Takeover Panel

- contractual obligations, such as the provisions of listing agreements (the so-called Purple Book for the UK's main market) with the market on which the company's shares are listed (in the UK, the FSA acts as the listing authority for the London Stock Exchange)

- codes of practice for directors, such as the UK Financial Reporting Council's Combined Code

- accounting standards and informal but often powerful controls exercised by investor and public opinion on matters such as the pay of the CEO (invariably too high) and of workers in poor countries (invariably too low)

- the environment, and social and community responsibility.

As the guardians of a company's assets, directors are expected to act with care and good faith in discharging their responsibilities. The UK Companies Act 2006 is being implemented over two years. It places new duties on all directors including the promotion of the company's success, the exercise of independent judgment and avoiding conflicts of interest.

The law relating to directors does not distinguish between executive and non-executive directors (NEDs). NEDs are rarely involved in the day-to-day running of the business, but they are equally responsible for the board's actions. If found to have acted unlawfully, NEDs can be disqualified for up to 15 years from holding directorships in the same way as executive directors.

The Combined Code, which incorporates many of the recommendations of the 2002 government-sponsored Higgs *Review of the Role and Effectiveness of Non-executive Directors*, requires NEDs to scrutinize and monitor the reporting of management performance, "satisfy themselves on the integrity of financial information," and ensure "financial controls and systems of risk management are robust and defensible." NEDS have a duty to restrain, or endeavor to dismiss, executive directors, if they believe they are acting improperly or underperforming, and they usually chair important board committees such as the audit committee and the remuneration committee. Since it's not now considered good practice for the positions of CEO and chair of the board to be occupied by the same person, non-executive chairmen or chairwomen are becoming almost universal in the UK, although not yet in the US.

Reading material

Thanks largely to the intense scrutiny of corporate governance after a crop of corporate scandals during the past decade or so, you will not be short of reading material. The Sarbanes-Oxley Act, passed by the US Senate in January 2002, is well worth a scan, particularly if the board you want to join governs a company listed in the US or has control over any US businesses. The report by Sir Derek Higgs, *Review of the Role and Effectiveness of Non-executive Directors*, *The Combined Code on Corporate Governance*, published by the UK Financial Reporting Council (FRC) and regularly updated, and the *Tyson Report on the Recruitment and Development of Non-Executive Directors*, published in 2003 and commissioned by Laura Tyson, then Dean of London Business School, are also worth inclusion on the reading lists of aspiring directors of UK companies.

Earlier reports, such as the Cadbury Report: *The Financial Aspects of Corporate Governance* (1992), the Greenbury Report: *On Directors' Remuneration* (1995), Sir Ronald Hempel's *Report of The Committee on Corporate Governance* (1998) and the Turnbull Report: *Internal Control: Guidance for Directors on the Combined Code* (1999), have all contributed to the evolution of the UK's codes of corporate governance.

Essential info is available in the regularly updated booklet *Guidance for Boardroom Practice* (apply to the Institute of Directors). In addition to sound advice and information on new developments relating to boards and their directors, it includes an alarmingly long list of statutes relating to the responsibilities and liabilities of UK directors. In addition to the Companies Acts, these include the Company Directors' Disqualification Act 1986, the Insolvency Act 1986, the Criminal Justice Act 1993, which made insider dealing a criminal offence, the Health and Safety at Work Act 1974, and the Environmental Protection Act 1990. *The Guide for Non-executive Directors,* by Hanson Green and the international law firm, Ashurst, is updated at regular intervals and is a mine of useful information for aspiring NEDs.[4] The booklet includes a diagram showing the various and varied roles of a NED, reproduced here as Figure 3.1.

Books, such as *Developing Directors* by Colin Coulson-Thomas[5] and *The Fish Rots from the Head* by Bob Garratt,[6] contain many useful

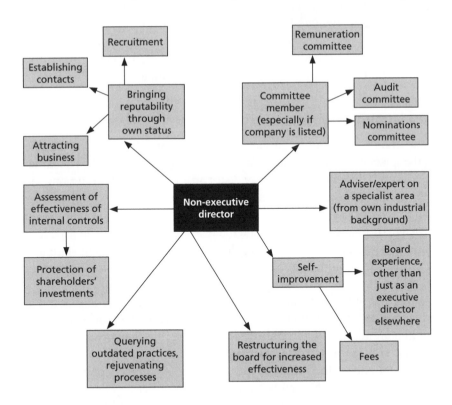

Figure 3.1 The role of a non-executive director

Source: Reproduced with permission of Hanson Green

insights and general, sometimes provocative overviews. Websites and newsletters, such as Betty Thayer's *The Non-Executive Director*, with an informative membership website at non-execs.com, and E-governance (www.governance.co.uk), will help users to keep abreast of developments in corporate governance.

Training and development

The UK's Institute of Directors offers a range of programs, from a one-day introduction, to a certificate, diploma and finally the chartered director qualification; headhunters, such as Spencer Stuart and Odgers Ray & Berndtson, run bespoke courses for both new and aspiring directors (executive and non-executive) and a browse on the web produces numerous hits on NED courses, programs, seminars, master classes and so on offered by universities and business schools all over the world.

Much can also be learned about the formal and legal framework within which all directors operate from serving on the boards of charities, smaller companies or public sector organizations, conversations with existing directors, male and female, coaching, and from the chairmen/mentors on the FTSE 100 Cross-Company Mentoring Programme.

Board language

A client of one of the authors, a successful lawyer, was having some trouble with the finance director on the board she had just joined. Perhaps because, like Winston Churchill with Nancy Astor in the House of Commons, he felt threatened by her, he appeared to see it as his mission in life to put her down on every possible occasion. His most potent weapon was his deep knowledge of finance. Whenever she made a suggestion about an aspect of the business she knew about, he would fix her with a withering stare and explain, as if to a child, that the finances didn't add up and so her proposal wouldn't create value for shareholders.

He was one of those detail-oriented FDs who see their role as that of the board's truth teller – the director who keeps his feet on the ground while all about him are looking at the stars. It's a valuable role in many ways, but if taken too far it can be very destructive.

The client solved the problem with the help of some coaching and the support of the CEO, who had been instrumental in her appointment to the board. She developed some anti-patronizing strategies and the FD had to back off. But she'd learned an important lesson; that she got out of her depth too quickly on finance.

The language of boards is legal and financial. In recent years, moral and social issues have attracted more attention at board level, but an understanding of company law and finance is still essential for a board candidate. Contrary to the popular view, sometimes encouraged by the finance function, finance isn't rocket science. Concepts such as shareholder value and the cost of capital are not hard to grasp. Women must master the financial details and support conclusions with data and analysis. There's plenty of help available. Most leading UK and US business schools run short courses on finance for executives with non-financial backgrounds. London Business School, for example, runs an intensive five-day residential "financial seminar for senior managers" four times a year.

Reflections for companies

It is clearly in the interests of companies to ensure that all their senior executives become progressively more legally and financially literate as they rise through the ranks. If company leaders want to appoint more women to their boards, they must try to ensure that the processes by which such literacy is acquired are open to all and not effectively reserved for men by long-standing conventions, or hidden prejudices about who needs it and from what functions credible board candidates will emerge.

Tutorials on governance, the legal responsibilities of directors and corporate finance can be arranged for invited senior executives, but make sure the invitees reflect the existing gender mix in middle and senior management. Patrons, sponsors and mentors must be assigned on a similarly even-handed basis. Since women may be less inclined than men to apply for training in this area, company leaders should make a particular point of encouraging their senior female executives to learn about corporate governance, board committee structure, company law, financial analysis, and so on.

Governance self-test

Professor Bob Garratt, visiting professor at Cass Business School in London, professor extraordinaire at the University of Stellenbosch Business School in South Africa, and an international consultant in board evaluation and development, has kindly composed some questions on current UK legislation and regulations to test readers' knowledge of UK corporate governance. The answers are provided at the end.

Questions:

1. The 2006 Companies Act consolidated centuries of legislation. What collective name does it give to the seven key director's duties?

2. If I use the term "director," but I have not signed Form 288A to be registered as a statutory director of my company, do I have the same liabilities as a statutory director?

3. In a limited liability company are directors covered by the liability limitation?

4. If a person frequently attends board meetings, joins in the discussions and influences decisions, but is not a statutory director, does he or she have any directorial liabilities?

5. Many not-for-profit organizations are registering as companies limited by guarantee, as well as being registered charities. Do directors of such companies have the same Companies Act duties and liabilities as all other directors?

6. The government is creating many director roles in the public services, including the NHS. Do these directors also have the same legal duties and liabilities as statutory directors?

7. It is becoming common for boards, committees and individual directors to be evaluated annually. Is this a requirement of the Companies Act 2006?

Answers:

1. The seven non-exhaustive duties.

2. Only statutory directors can use the term "director." It's very dangerous to use such terms as "assistant director," or "director of ..." if the person is not a statutory director, because they would be committing the offence of holding themselves out to be something they are not and, moreover, would not be covered by the directors' liability insurance policy.

3. No. The limitation of liability is only on shareholder's paid-up capital. Directors have unlimited liability, which is why it is wise to have a liability insurance policy, even though it cannot cover all eventualities.

4. Yes. The courts would usually treat him or her as a shadow director, with the same liabilities and insurance implications as in question 2.

5. Yes.

6. No one knows. Their legal status isn't clear. Best practice is to behave as if they do.

7. No, but it is a requirement of the 2003 Combined Code of corporate governance. This only applies to listed companies, but it is considered best practice for all companies.

References

1. *An Inquiry into the Nature and Causes of the Wealth of Nations*, Adam Smith, Ward, Lock and Tyler, 1776.
2. *The Modern Corporation and Private Property*, Adolph Berle and Gardiner Means, Macmillan, 1933.
3. *Power without Property: A New Development in American Political Economy*, Adolph Berle, Harcourt Brace, 1959.
4. *The Guide for Non-executive Directors*, Hanson Green and Ashurst, designed and produced by Spring O'Brien, London, 2006.
5. *Developing Directors, A Guidebook for Building an Effective Boardroom Team*, Colin Coulson-Thomas, www.policypublications.com/developingdirectors.htm.
6. *Thin On Top: Why Corporate Governance Matters*, Bob Garratt, Nicholas Brealey, 2003; *The Fish Rots from the Head*, Bob Garratt, Profile Books, 2003.

CHAPTER 4

The unwritten rules

A board is an organism not a process: the more you understand that, and show you understand it, the more attractive a potential director you are likely to be.

Baroness Hogg, chairman, 3i plc

Imagine you're climbing the vertical element of a "T." There comes a point, a "hinge moment," when you emerge from the vertical and enter the horizontal. This is what happens when you emerge from the top of your functional silo into the board milieu. Your horizons abruptly broaden.

C-level executives (CEO, CFO, COO, and so on), to whom you are

© Barbara Shore

THE T-STEP

accustomed to report, are now your peers, with whom you must become accustomed to sharing decision-making and responsibility.

The board basics constitute the formal framework and language of the board. But that's just one of the dimensions of the much wider space you have just entered. As you stand poised on the board threshold, look around, attune your senses and emotions, and try to get a feel for the social dynamics operating within the formal framework. Think deeply about and try to anticipate how your own personality and gender will affect those dynamics.

Unwritten rules and norms operate in the board milieu that are quite different from those that apply lower down the hierarchy. Women who aspire to board positions must study the conventions and adapt their behavior accordingly. How you conduct yourself in the board milieu will shape your image and thus your apparent suitability for a board appointment.

It is important for women to recognize at the outset that this board milieu, this social anteroom of boards (places and situations where board candidates get together, socialize, network, and put themselves about) is essentially political and essentially male. The arrival of the first woman (and to a somewhat lesser extent, the second and the third) is quite likely, therefore, to have an effect on the resident men not unlike the effect Nancy Astor's arrival in the British House of Commons in 1919 had on Winston Churchill (see Chapter 2).

We will begin this chapter by investigating why women sometimes find it difficult to settle in easily and quickly to the board milieu. It is not because of overt or deliberate resistance by men. It's simply that men are used to running things in their own male ways, and will themselves often find it hard to adapt to what amounts to, for them, the arrival of an alien in their midst, who does not take their male ways for granted. Women must understand that and enter the political board game with their eyes open.

Enter the alien

In a 2007 article in the *Harvard Business Review*, Alice Eagly and Linda Carli suggested that the concept of the "glass ceiling" was outdated, because the problem for women aspiring to high office these days is not that there's an invisible barrier denying them access to the top echelon. Rather it is that they encounter various subtle and not so subtle obstacles throughout their careers, which push them off the career ladder at a roughly similar rate at every level. As a result, disproportionately few women enter the board milieu and become board candidates.[1]

They suggest that, for these reasons, the "labyrinth" – a barrier of

© Barbara Shore

ENTER THE ALIEN

complexity, rather than impermeability – is a more appropriate image than the glass ceiling for the problems facing women aspiring to high office.

Two of the labyrinthine obstacles women face, according to Eagly and Carli, are resistance to female leadership in general and to women's leadership styles, in particular. As we noted in our first book – citing Eagly's own meta-analysis – numerous studies have shown that people associate men and women with different traits, and that they associate leadership with male traits. That means that playing the game the same way as men will not work for women. Women are not seen as being authentically female when they exhibit the qualities, such as aggression, ambition, dominance, self-reliance, and individualism, people associate with leadership. If, on the other hand, they behave in ways people associate with women – if they're affectionate, kind, friendly, sensitive, and soft-spoken – they're not considered to have the right stuff for a leadership position.

Annoyingly, this "double bind," as Eagly and Carli call it, does not appear to apply to men. Various studies have shown that while female leaders are scorned for being ambitious and aggressive, male leaders are admired for being warm and friendly. But it's not even as simple as that. Another aspect of the double bind was neatly illustrated by Senator Hillary Clinton when giving the Mary Louise Smith lecture at the Carrie Chapman Catt Center for Women and Politics in October 2007. She recalled a newspaper agony column she'd read in the early 1980s. A reader had asked: "I'm about to get a big promotion and I'm going to have my own office for the first time. What kinds of decorations are appropriate for my office?" The columnist wanted to know if the writer was a man or a woman. If the questioner was a man with a family, he was advised to display pictures of his family, because people will think "this is a stable person with a good set of family values." If the questioner was a woman, however, she shouldn't put up pictures of her family, because people will think she can't keep her mind on the job.

Even more annoying is the fact that the full deployment of female traits in a leadership role seems to produce better leadership, despite the fact that female traits are not generally seen as leadership traits. This paradoxical result emerged from Eagly's earlier analysis, which distinguished between *transactional* and *transformational* leadership. The former rewards and punishes to appeal to the subordinate's self-interest. The latter mentors and encourages subordinates to realize their potential. The analysis found that the transformational style delivered better individual and organizational performance, and that female leaders were somewhat more transformational than men.

Margaret Heffernan, entrepreneur and writer, believes that women are employing a new and, by implication at any rate, improved leadership paradigm. In an interview on BBC Radio 4, she said:

> These ways of working suggest that the old corporate notions – of business as war, of companies as machines, and of leadership as command – don't work for women ... [They're] more interested in orchestration, empathy and relationship management.[2]

The differences and, to some extent, the tensions between what could be loosely characterized as the female and male styles of leadership are being openly discussed in the media these days. In an interview with Greg Hurst, political correspondent of *The Times*, at the end of 2007, Tessa Jowell, who had been a minister in Tony Blair's government, called on Gordon Brown, Tony Blair's successor as UK prime minister, to change his style:

The most important thing for any prime minister is to be authentic and to be yourself and I think Gordon Brown should feel complete freedom to be himself ... What people want in modern leaders is to know them, not necessarily to like them ... but to know them.

Jowell, who had urged ministers in the past to show more "emotional intelligence," went on:

We [the Labour Party] have to relate much more to the core values, to the attitudes people have to the things that matter to [them] ... You have to stand firm; you have to be confident. Confidence is born of making decisions with care, taking people with you, believing that you have exercised the best judgment on the basis of the best available advice and taking a decision that you believe is consistent with [your] values and beliefs.[3]

We mention this research and Tessa Jowell's views on leadership, not as a prelude to offering a resolution of the tension nor as a way out of the double bind, but to illustrate the impact that the arrival of the first woman may have on the social dynamics of the board milieu. The research suggests the aspiring female director must find some way to seem authentic and true to herself and her gender and, at the same time, project leadership qualities. One mentee on our program said:

One of the issues for me is that I've seen a lot of unproductive board behavior, so the role models around are not always the best ones. The challenge is to find a way to operate effectively within a culture functioning in a certain way, without resorting to precisely the kinds of behaviors making it dysfunctional in the first place.

It is generally assumed that female leadership styles reflect female traits; that men and women lead in a different ways, in business and in politics, because men and women are different. But there might be another explanation for such differences.

Citing research that found women leaders are more participative and collaborative than male leaders, Eagly and Carli say the difference "is unlikely to be genetic. Rather, it may be that collaboration can get results without seeming particularly masculine." As they puzzle out the mysteries of the labyrinth, women try "to project authority without ... [using the autocratic style] that people find so jarring in women."

Although Eagly and Carli don't explore it in their *HBR* article, this is an intriguing idea. Could it be that successful women leaders employ collaborative and transformational styles of leadership not because they're women and not because such styles are more effective than the transactional styles used by men (although they seem to be, in the modern business environment), but because the labyrinth acts as a Darwinian natural selector of leadership styles and has, so far at any rate, rejected women who employ other styles?

If this is what has been happening, it's important, because it means that the question of what's the best style for the aspiring female leader remains open. The business environment may change and select other leadership styles. The labyrinth may change, as more women enter the board milieu and the current link between leadership and male traits gradually weakens. The important point here is that aspiring leaders of both genders must understand the different criteria the labyrinth uses to select male and female leadership styles and adapt their own styles accordingly. They must also recognize that although there are labyrinths in all organizations, their selection criteria may change over time and will differ from one organization to another.

As the selection criteria for board members change, the board itself will change. Sir Philip Hampton, chairman of J Sainsbury, is in no doubt about the inherent plasticity of boards, and the power of new members to change them. He told us:

> There are unwritten rules of engagement, but new people will always be writing new ones. In a sense, women coming onto boards is all about that. It's not as if the rules were established in the 1950s and can't change subsequently. Anybody coming onto a board should have the sense that they can make a new contribution; you're not just there to blend into the background of the normal behavior. You can change content and direction. You have to feel that you are giving something new.

Common mistakes

Whether the reason for the differences in male and female leadership styles is innate, or the product of labyrinth selection, it is clear that women who aspire to high office must think carefully about what leadership styles to adopt and the constraints imposed on their choice by the double bind.

Some women try too hard; some are too diffident; some don't transmit the signals that they want to be in the game; some are uncomfortable with the macho language; some adopt styles and personae that make it hard for others to work with them.

"Women are either too soft or they're hectoring, and find it hard to find the middle ground," said one of our mentees. That's because the middle ground is hard to find. "I always have trouble with the word 'ambition,'" said another mentee. "It puts me in mind of people who are ruthless, aggressive and completely out for themselves." And yet the same woman was accused by a male colleague in another department of being bullying and high-handed.

This is the double bind. No wonder some ambitious women feel they're damned if they do adopt a certain style, and damned if they don't.

Their dilemma is exacerbated by their dislike of boasting, and their aversion to risk-taking, created by their fear of failure. They tend to see politics as something you do to, rather than with, people; as insincere and sucking up; as tacky.

The importance women attach to their relationships with other people can also become a weakness, in company politics, where alliances and coalitions are coalescing and breaking up more or less continuously. After two men have a stand-up row in public, they may have a drink in the pub together. Women take arguments much more personally. They're reluctant to argue openly, even about issues that they feel strongly about, because they feel that a public row with a colleague could do irreparable damage to the relationship. This is particularly true of relationships between women. There's a solidarity point here. As one senior woman executive put it to us:

> You don't want people to think that the only two women at the top don't get on, so you often don't confront issues with other senior women in the same way as you would with senior men.

This negative attitude to politics makes many women reluctant to use their *personal*, as opposed to their *positional* power. They feel that using personal power – charm, wit, personality, poise – at work is somehow illegitimate. So they try to maximize their positional power by doing their own jobs exceptionally well. They put themselves at a disadvantage, however, when they eschew the use of personal power, because men have no such reservations about using their personal power. We know very few top businesspeople, men or women, who aren't exceptionally charming, amusing, and sticklers for etiquette (see box opposite).

Perhaps some people are born more charming than others. There may be a gene, or set of genes, that codes for charm and predisposes some people to develop the quality. It's clear to us, however, that there is nothing to prevent those who lack the charm gene, if it exists, from developing the quality. Able men and women who set their sights on leadership roles work hard at developing charm, because they soon realize that it's one of the necessary qualities for entering the political and social labyrinths they must negotiate successfully if they're to get to the top. Those who lack charm and good manners rarely make it to the top, because these deficiencies prevent them from forming the coalitions and alliances needed to pave the way.

Those charmless few who do make it to the top don't tend to last. When the CEO of a major UK company was recently forced from office by his board, it was said that he possessed all the qualities necessary in a leader except charm.

Etiquette: Some dos and don'ts

A lot of this is about remembering and abiding by the rules you were taught when you were young, but which, in the bustle and pressure of contemporary business life, you may sometimes forget or overlook.

1. Write those "thank you" letters for help given to you or kindness shown to you.

2. Don't inadvertently be rude. Don't just observe the courtesies; be courteous and well mannered always.

3. Try to be tactful.

4. Do not be sarcastic or sardonic.

5. Show respect for others by being punctual: being late is a theft of other people's time.

6. Return phone calls and emails as promptly as possible.

7. Treat others with respect as equal human beings.

8. If you feel you're being attacked or patronized (like the woman whose predicament we described in Chapter 3) don't respond in kind. Wait for the second beat, and deal with the comment in an adult-to-adult manner.

9. Show genuine empathy for others and the issues they're facing; be supportive, but not intrusive.

Basic principles

It is easier said than done, of course, but the trick in politics is to be yourself, rather than a woman playing a man's game:

- Don't take yourself too seriously

- Keep your antennae up for common ground when talking with other players; be interested and interesting

- Develop a repertoire of topics you can talk about fluently, such as hobbies or outside interests

- Don't be afraid to use your charm, empathy and courtesy.

An irony here is that women tend to be more socially adept than men. If they would only use their superior social skills, women would have an enormous advantage over men in corporate politics.

In an article in *You* magazine, "The new charm offensive," the author argued that some women business leaders had started to exploit their gender's superior social skills. Thanks to "the new breed of female high flyers ... a non-confrontational, humane style" of management is being established and "the macho world of business is slowly coming to its senses and has realised that playing hard ball is passé."[4]

Sure, politics sometimes has a seedy side, but looked at differently using a different language, it can appear in a more positive light. Think of it as influencing, alliance-building, diplomacy or creating awareness. Think of it as necessary, because, paraphrasing Churchill on democracy, it is the worst way of assigning power in a company or other organisation, except all those other ways that have been tried from time to time.

You must find ways to make politics palatable or even enjoyable. You don't have to play the political game the same way men play it – you can develop your own style, which plays to your strengths – but play it you must, if the board's your destination.

Networking

Networking is an integral part of politics and is vital in the board milieu. Eagly and Carli suggest in their *HBR* article and their book, *Through the Labyrinth,*[5] that one of the reasons so few women achieve leadership positions in business is their "underinvestment in social capital." In other words, for whatever reason, women spend much less time than men networking, and time spent networking has been found to correlate closely with hierarchy-climbing speed.

One problem for women, of course, is that the networking they devote insufficient time to has, hitherto, and partly, no doubt, because so few women have engaged in it, been male oriented – pubs, sport and sport-related events (track days, hunting, soccer matches, and so on) and in the evenings in some cases, in some industries, lap-dancing clubs and Hooters restaurants (a US restaurant chain, where the waitresses are called Hooters girls). Although by no means universal, these are typical venues and events for male networking. It is not just that women find them somewhat less than irresistible; it is also that they don't fit in there. Their presence cramps the men's style and robs the occasions of their essential informality. Moreover, the timing – evenings and weekends – is often inconvenient for women. As one of our mentees put it: "on weekday evenings my first priority is supervising my son's homework."

It gets much more civilized at senior levels. Ascot and Glyndebourne are substituted for Twickenham and Soho. By then, however, much of the damage for women will have been done. The relationships imported into the more cultured networking in the board milieu will have been forged earlier, often in less refined, exclusively male settings.

There is not much an individual woman can do about this male bonding tradition in professional networking, apart from coming up with some suggestions for less male-oriented socializing – dinner parties at home or in town, concerts, family get-togethers. As more women reach senior executive level, of course, pressure will grow for a shift to more gender-neutral bonding sessions. In the meantime, dedicate some time in your diary to networking and don't delete it.

But networking is much more than mere socializing. In essence, it is establishing and maintaining personal, as opposed to professional, relationships with colleagues and associates, and it is based on the principle of reciprocity.

Reciprocity theory

Numerous examples of cooperative behaviour in nature were, for many years, a puzzle for evolution theorists. It was easy to explain the care of parents for their young; they were maximizing the chances of survival of carriers of their own genes. But kinship theory didn't explain how cooperation evolved between unrelated animals. Why, for example, do unrelated gulls peck parasites from each other's necks? The gulls benefit from the practice, because they can't reach their own necks with their beaks, but how could this instinct have evolved among carriers of selfish genes?

The answer, which came to be known as "reciprocity theory," was that the gulls' mutual pecking is not unconditional. A gull will peck the neck of a stranger, but it will recognize that stranger and will not peck its neck again if it cheats – takes a free ride – and doesn't return the favor. The ability to spot cheaters is so important that natural selection has reserved a relatively large area of the gull's brain for recognition – for distinguishing between reciprocators and cheaters.

We carry the reciprocity gene too. Society is its expression. In our dealings with one another, we also distinguish between reciprocators and cheaters. References to the idea of reciprocity and the implicit bargains that people strike with each other crop up frequently in our art and literature. In the end, the value you get out of networking is equal to the value you give. It is from webs of reciprocal favors and obligations that patron/ protégé and mentor/mentee relationships and, more generally, political coalitions and alliances emerge. Men have no advantage in this kind of relationship-building and maintenance. If anything, it is women, with their greater warmth, friendliness and sensitivity, who have the edge. But our networking is not an immediate return system. The good networker doesn't do someone a favor in the expectation of it being returned in kind at a specified date. It is not a series of discrete deals; not "You peck my neck; I'll peck yours." It is more "As you sow; so shall you reap"; a form of socializing that, although ultimately based on reciprocity, has no particular goal in mind; just an expectation that, in the end, a series of favors given will lead to a series of favors returned.

This is familiar territory for women. When Kate, friend of one of the authors, died suddenly in summer 2007, an informal, but powerful and well-resourced support network consisting of her son's friends and their parents immediately swung into action to help Josh and father James adapt to their new situation. Sleepovers and trips were organized, school pickups were scheduled and various backup arrangements were made available, should they be needed. The fathers helped, but it was the mothers, with their deep sympathy and acute empathy, who organized and energized the system. They had made it their business to know what was needed, and when. After James and Josh had reconfigured and stabilized their lives, James sent flowers to thank them.

Business networks are just the same. They generate goodwill for the thoughtful, reciprocating networker among colleagues and associates, including suppliers and customers, that provides political power and influence and what can become invaluable support in difficult times.

Lessons from a master

Empathy is crucial in professional networks, too. There is a passage in Alastair Campbell's diaries[6] describing a visit to London in July 2003 by ex-US President Bill Clinton. Campbell was Prime Minister Tony Blair's press secretary at the time. He and his boss were both up against it. Campbell was engaged in a bad-tempered row with the BBC (British Broadcasting Corporation) over the allegation, by a BBC reporter, that the government had "sexed up" intelligence reports on Saddam Hussein's so-called weapons of mass destruction, to provide a *casus belli* for the invasion of Iraq. Blair himself was being sniped at by anti-war members of the Parliamentary Labour Party (PLP) – his own MPs.

After lunch at the Ritz, which Blair couldn't attend, Campbell asked Clinton what he thought of his and Blair's problems. He was rewarded with what Campbell called "a masterclass in political strategy."

Clinton urged Campbell to develop a new strategy for the PLP and try to

> understand their lives. You guys go to DC [Washington]. You have real power. They get weekends in their constituencies ... It's about their psychology. It's the same with the press. Some you will never win, but others you will, if you're nice to them, involve them. Your MPs know TB [Tony Blair] is better than them, but that doesn't mean they are nothing ... People are falling out of love with Tony, because they think he has fallen out of love with them ... They know he has to do this other stuff, but they want to know he cares about them.

Use all of you

Whatever one thinks of his values, politics and sexual appetites, one has to acknowledge that Bill Clinton was and remains the consummate politician and influencer. The above quotes include valuable lessons for those who aspire to high office. First, relationships transcend position. Although he'd left the White House, Clinton still saw Blair and Campbell as members of his network. Second, empathy is the main foundation of successful networking. He advised Campbell to imagine what it was like to be a rank-and-file MP or a journalist (to "walk in the other person's moccasins," as we would say), because he had to understand where the hostile journalists and disgruntled MPs were coming from, before he could mend broken fences and bruised relationships. Third, practical politics has as much to do with diplomacy as power-broking. Clinton is the consummate diplomat, because he's fascinated by, and an acute reader of, social dynamics and he knows it is vital to keep talking.

Fourth, and most important of all, deploy all your personality. Read the group dynamics and then use your charm, wit, charisma, gravitas, poise, and any other qualities you have at your disposal to influence people in a way that suits you. Clinton did.

There is another lesson from Clinton in Campbell's diaries. It's not enough to work out where other people are coming from. You also need to look inside yourself and understand your own emotional state (see Chapter 8). In what Campbell believed was a reference to the Monica Lewinsky affair, Clinton opened up and said:

My brother was a cocaine addict and the word to remember for addicts is HALT. Yes it means stop. But it also means I'm Hungry, I'm Angry, Lonely and Tired ... I wasn't hungry, but I was angry, lonely and tired. I was being beaten up by everyone. Ken Starr [of the Starr Report, which led to Clinton's impeachment for perjury and obstruction of justice in December 1998] was trying to put me in jail. Friends were leaving me and enemies were killing me. Hillary was angry with me. This ball of fire came at me ... I felt H, A, L, T.

But he didn't let it get to him. He was acquitted of the impeachment charges by the Senate in February 1999 and emerged from his various trials and tribulations with his reputation as being one of the most talented politicians of his time intact. His success and resilience, we believe, was because he came over as an able and charismatic, but flawed, human being, rather than as an unimpeachable president. This is the point. Bill Clinton would have been less of a president and a politician if he had brought to the job less than all of himself.

This need to bring all of yourself to the table means that effective communication on non-business matters is very important in the board milieu. Talking to others in the board milieu about your daughter's plans to swim the Bristol Channel, your son's art exhibition or your own interest in medieval London, for example, helps you to make what we call "finger-tip contact" as one human being with another. Talking person to person in this way, rather than business associate to business associate, builds trust and facilitates empathy. If there's anywhere where you should deploy your personality fully, and "to be that self that one truly is," as Carl Rogers put it,[7] it is surely in the place where the realizations of your career dreams and potential are almost within your grasp.

Meetings in the milieu

It's not all networking and small talk in the board milieu. There is business to be done too. But because there's more power and politics above the silo tops in the board milieu, more subtle group dynamics, more hidden agendas, broader concerns and implications, the business is done in a different way.

Women new to board meetings are often surprised to find that they're being asked formally to approve decisions already made informally in corridor conversations in which they were not involved. They must get used to this kind of activity, engage in informal canvassing and lobbying, and seize opportunities for chats about important issues before such issues reach the board.

They must also deploy their emotional intelligence in their dealings with people in and around board and executive committee meetings.

The client we mentioned in Chapter 3, who had trouble with the finance director on her first board, realized she needed to know more about finance. She realized something else, too; that since she couldn't change his behavior, she would have to change hers. Instead of feeling wrong-footed, undermined and angry with the FD (which was doubtless apparent from her facial expression and body language), she adopted a new strategy, to retain her poise and equanimity and to be constantly delightful (to use her charm, in other words). She also adopted a new stratagem for dealing with the FD. Instead of counterattacking when he sniped at her in board meetings, she put her hands together, steepled her fingertips, pressed them to her lips, looked thoughtful and said: "I'm concerned about ... ." The effect was all she had hoped for – the FD was nonplussed, and the attention of the rest of the board switched to her and what she was concerned about.

Successful politicians, diplomats and business executives do quite a bit of this sort of acting, because they know that there is a lot of the theatre in high-level meetings. They're not trying to be someone else; they are responding, with emotional intelligence, to the group dynamics and exerting influence on those dynamics. You should try to build support; to get people on your side; to help them to realize they enjoy being with you, or that people tend to be calmer when you are present. Your aim is to get others to want you to participate in the debates. You must be polite, without being weak. You need tough-mindedness, what we call "musculature," and Clintonesque resilience; when you're knocked down, you have to get up and dust off your knees. Keep telling yourself, as the mother of one of the authors told her after a setback, "there is nothing here you can't deal with." But as a mentee said, you do need "sharper elbows" when operating at board level. Our chairmen mentors agree. One said admiringly of his mentee: "she's tough."

As you approach board level, you need to learn how to analyze what is happening in meetings and interpret the unfolding dynamics. You have to notice and divine the significance of "the dog that didn't bark," as Sherlock Holmes would put it; of silences or momentary pauses; of glances passed between individuals. Do they indicate an alliance, or are they signals of some kind? Effective executives have learned to deconstruct the group dynamics in meetings quickly to enable them to intervene effectively. These aren't gender-related skills – some men are brilliant at this, and others don't have a clue. The problem for women is that they've usually had fewer chances to observe and study gifted practitioners of their own gender.

It takes time and dedication to learn to read people accurately, but there are three basic principles:

■ Slow down

■ Pay close attention; listen carefully; watch intently

■ Say less; make what you do say weigh more.

It is also vital to be open to feedback. This is much more important than training and development courses. Feedback can teach you about yourself and about the effectiveness of your style and stratagems in the board milieu. Your curiosity about what other people are feeling should include a curiosity about what they are feeling and thinking about you.

Feedback provides the self-awareness you need, if you are to project the three Cs – confidence, competence, contribution – that one of our mentors says he particularly values in a NED. We will return to the issues of feedback, reflection and self-awareness in Chapter 8.

Reflections for companies

A company leader who wishes to appoint a woman to his main board for the first time, but has no immediate plans to do so, might usefully think about how welcoming the organization as a whole, and its board in particular, will appear to a woman. How many senior executives are women? What's the attrition rate of women at each management level? In other words, how hard are his senior female executives finding it to negotiate the organization's labyrinth?

What formal and informal selection criteria are being used to screen candidates for high office? Are they appropriate, or do they reflect outdated assumptions about the personality traits of leaders? What systems are used for senior appointments? Are there any women on the selection board, or any men who've already appointed women to senior positions?

In a recent experiment at a leading bank, the members of a promotion board agreed to the recording of their conversations. Why would they not? They had nothing to hide. They would just be doing their usual, even-handed, gender-neutral job, and were happy to be recorded. They quickly forgot about the microphones and got on with the interviews. The subsequent analysis revealed that their conversation had focused exclusively on the "stars" (their name for the best candidates) and the "rubbish" (the no-hopers). The candidates who were neither stars nor rubbish, which included most of the female candidates (maybe because they lacked traits people usually associate with leadership) weren't discussed at all.

In one case, a candidate for a senior sales job was described, by one selection board member, as a "real animal." In the context, this was a term of approbation. The candidate could not conceivably have been a woman, because, had she been, "real animal" would clearly not have been a compliment, quite the contrary, and would have made no sense.

There's prejudice embedded in this kind of language that needs to be acknowledged and eradicated. Members of that promotion board realize that now. They were genuinely surprised and dismayed when confronted by the results of an analysis of the taped promotion session. All of them were men, but they were trying hard to create a level playing field for women in their bank. They were convinced, when they agreed to the taping of their discussions, that the analysis would reveal a gender-blind assessment of each candidate on his or her merits.

Company leaders should also listen very closely to the language used in the networking that occurs in the board milieu. Does it or could it accommodate women or is it so male oriented that women entrants to the board milieu are effectively excluded?

To some this may sound prissy. Boys will be boys. It's just harmless fun; just street banter. But that misses the point. Once women enter the board milieu, it's not just boys any more. The board milieu must adapt to accommodate women. There's nothing harmless about it if the ambience of the board milieu excludes women. As more women join the board milieu, of course, pressure will grow for a shift towards more gender-neutral socializing sessions.

Company leaders considering the appointment of a particular woman to their boards for the first time should ask themselves two questions: What's the impact of her arrival on the existing board likely to be? How is she likely to react to, and how well will she be able to operate within, the existing board ambience? Boards change when one director retires or another joins, and previously male-only boards change disproportionately when the first woman joins, and again when the second and third women join. Company leaders should do what they can to ensure these inevitable changes turn out to be for the better and that a genuinely gender-neutral board ambience is given a chance to emerge.

References

1.   "Women and the labyrinth of leadership," Alice Eagly and Linda Carli, *Harvard Business Review*, September, 2007.

2. *Women Change the Rules of Business*, John Byrne, producer of BBC Radio 4's *Changing the Rules*, August 13, 2007. See also *The Naked Truth: A Working Woman's Manifesto on Business and What Really Matters*, Margaret Heffernan, Jossey-Bass, 2004.
3. "Ministers urge Brown to change leadership style as Tory poll lead slips," *The Times*, December 31, 2007.
4. "The new charm offensive," *You, Mail on Sunday*, October 7, 2007.
5. *Through the Labyrinth: The Truth about how Women Become Leaders*, Alice Eagly and Linda Carli, Harvard Business School Press, 2007.
6. *The Blair Years: Extracts from the Alastair Campbell Diaries*, Alastair Campbell, Hutchinson, 2007.
7. *On Becoming a Person: A Therapist's View of Psychotherapy*, Carl Rogers, Constable, 1961.

CHAPTER 5

A sense of direction

You need to be clear what your unique competitive advantage is, and target the companies that need that quality.

Richard Olver, chairman, BAE Systems plc

Ambition and aspirations gain power and energy when they become more specific. The wish to be successful by itself provides no guidance for action. To be successful at what, or as what? To be successful tomorrow, the day after or in five years' time? And what do you mean by success? How will you know when you're successful?

The wish to join a board is certainly more specific than the wish to be successful, but not much more. What kind of board – a subsidiary board or a main board? What kind of director – executive or non-executive? By when do you want to be, for example, a non-executive director on the main board of FTSE 100 company – by the time you're 40, 45 or 50 or after the children, if you have children, have left home?

A SENSE OF DIRECTION

To take the first step with confidence, you need to know where you're going. You need a reasonably well-specified aspiration and to derive from your aspiration a reasonably detailed plan for how you're going to realize it.

As Sir Philip Hampton, chairman of J Sainsbury, and a mentor on the FTSE Cross-Company Mentoring Programme, puts it:

> Setting targets is vital. "Joining a board" is an unfocused aspiration – you need to be focused.

Basic targeting

Having decided to engage, having accepted the need for some home-work on the board basics, and having surveyed and begun to acclimatize to the social dynamics of the board milieu, you need to give yourself a sense of direction.

You need to decide towards which board, in which industry someone like you – with your interests, experience, skills, aptitudes, values, and qualifica-tions – should be heading. And you need to try to work out which board or boards are most likely to be looking for someone like you. Since a perfect fit between your interests and credentials and the needs of the boards of organi-zations that attract you at any one time is too much to hope for, tradeoffs will be required. You need to optimize; to find the closest possible fit, given the constraints of what you can offer and what companies are looking for.

It's unlikely that any fit you find will be close enough to make you a good candidate for a particular vacancy right away, so you'll have to work at closing the gaps. We will come to the question of how to close gaps in Chapter 8. To start with, among the criteria for selecting a target, ask yourself how easy it is, and how long it will take to upgrade your existing personal capital to a level where you will be a good candidate for a board position at a company that interests and attracts you.

But don't assume that you must confine your targets to industries in which you have experience. Richard Olver, chairman of BAE Systems and also one of our mentors, says:

> They don't have to be in the same sector you are working in. Think of my mentee. She has a competitive advantage in the whole people and remuneration area. She could chair the Remco of a board in another sector. But you can't just appear somewhere with no advantage; with nothing that is special.

Sir Philip Hampton concurs: "You'll only be selected if a board thinks you have skills that match their needs."

Before discussing the criteria for selecting your provisional target companies or organizations, you should be clear about the status of your targets in your life plan. It's up to you how wedded you are to your target, but we suggest you shouldn't get fixated on it. The way we see it, its purpose is to give you an initial sense of direction, not to be a focus for all your efforts or the goal you pursue to the exclusion of all else. Be flexible enough to grasp any opportunities when they arise. Be ready to change target when circumstances change or chance encounters create unexpected openings. A target should be a compass that guides – not a straitjacket that precludes changes of course. Luck, which we define, in this context, as "the place where opportunity and preparation meet," plays an important part in career development. Be ready to ride the luck that comes your way. Ready! Fire! Aim! – where ready includes having provisional targets – should be your strategy.

Selection criteria: industries

Your interests and enthusiasms, your circumstances, your experiences and qualifications, your assessment of your aptitudes and abilities, and your inclinations may help you to separate industries into those that attract you and those that do not. You may, for example, like the idea of being a director of a retail group, but not wish to have anything to do with the tobacco industry or companies engaged in the arms trade. Your experience in marketing or your abiding fascination with brands may attract you to the fast moving consumer goods industry, but financial services may leave you cold, or vice versa.

If you want to be systematic about sector selection, you can give an industry a weighting to signify its attractiveness to you, and then use that weighting to discount any opportunities in that sector that come up. It's not usually a question of deciding between two or more opportunities, however. Sometimes they're like buses – you wait for years, and then two come along at once – but the decision is usually more like: "It's not exactly what I wanted, but it has a few things going for it. Should I take it, or wait for that other possibility I have had my eye on, which may or may not come up?"

Table 5.1, from *The Female FTSE Report 2007*, ranks the top 10 sectors represented in the FTSE 100 by the percentage of women on their main boards. The sample sizes are small and the rankings will change from year to year, so don't rely too much on these figures. And, more importantly, don't set too much store by industry stereotypes. They might not be true and even if there's something in them, there may not be as much as there once was.

It's widely thought, for example, that some industries are naturally more masculine than others. The mining and engineering industries are often cited as examples. Cynthia Carroll's appointment as CEO of Anglo American, the mining giant, in 2006 should help eventually to disabuse women and companies of such prejudices. But it may take a while. The stereotypes are deeply embedded.

TABLE 5.1 The top 10 female-friendly sectors	
Sector	Percentage women directors
Transport	27
Software	22
Investment	20
Food, drug and general retailers	17
Banks	14
Pharmaceuticals, health, personal care and household	14
Tobacco	13
Telecoms	13
Media & entertainment	13
Beverages	12

Source: Cranfield University School of Management

In an article in the *Sunday Times*[1] soon after the announcement of Carroll's appointment, Louise Armitstead reported that "the City was scandalised." "It's a woman," spluttered one analyst. "They'll never accept her," warned another. More concerned, perhaps, with giving the reporter a quotable quote than a dispassionate reaction to Carroll's appointment, he went on:

> Anglo is run by empire-builders at one end and bruising miners at the other. The appointment of a woman tea lady would be seen as too advanced by the first ... and a distraction by the others.

It could be argued that the putatively "blokey" industries and those at the bottom of the female-friendliness ranking in Table 5.1 are actually quite interesting for women seeking board positions, because, thanks partly to the negative publicity generated by their positions in the Female FTSE Report, they have further to go than other industries to reach the reputationally neutral zone at the female-friendly median.

Selection criteria: companies

Once you have your ranking of attractive industries, focus in on the main players. Are there any companies in your highly ranked sectors that, for whatever reason, you find particularly attractive? Keep an eye on them in the press and do some homework. Visit their websites, read their annual reports and their mission and value statements, if you can get hold of them. Try to get a sense of their cultures. Does it seem as if their values are aligned with yours?

Look closely at their boards. What is the gender balance? What's the split between executive and non-executive? How old is each director; are any going to be retiring in the near future? What's their provenance; in which areas of business are they working or were they working before their appointments? Look at their committee structures, particularly at the Nomcos; do they include any women and do they have any gender and diversity goals?

We believe (we would, wouldn't we?) that a useful criterion when you are assessing the accessibility of a particular main board to women is whether its chairman or CEO acts, or has acted, as a mentor in the FTSE 100 Cross-Company Mentoring Programme. The figures support this belief. An analysis of *The Female FTSE Report 2007* shows the average gender balance of the boards of FTSE 100 companies whose chairmen or CEOs are mentors on the program is 13.4 percent women (just under 12 percent in 2006), compared with 10.7 percent women (just over 9 percent in 2006) for the FTSE 100 as a whole. It seems possible that there is a causal connection between a relatively high proportion of women on a board and the participation of the chairman or CEO in the FTSE 100 Cross-Company Mentoring Programme. But it's hard to be sure which way round it is. Are the chairmen and CEOs of companies with better balanced boards more inclined to accept our invitations to join the program or do they become more inclined to appoint female directors as a result of being mentors? It's probably a bit of both, and if so, an interesting set of companies for women are those whose chairmen/CEOs are mentors on the program, but with relatively few or no women on their boards.

Take a look at the gender balance on executive committees too. Companies are not obliged to disclose this, but most FTSE 100 constituents do. According to Cranfield's *Female FTSE Report 2007*, 80 of the FTSE 100 constituents disclose the compositions of their executive committees on their websites or in their annual reports. These committees go by a variety of names, are chaired by the CEO, and include the executive directors and other senior executives who are, almost by definition, executive directors in waiting. As *The Female FTSE Report 2007* says, the non-director members of the executive committees "are a resource pool for future main board directorships."

An analysis of *The Female FTSE Report 2007* showed the average gender balance of executive committees of FTSE 100 companies that disclose such membership and whose chairmen or CEOs are mentors on the program is 10.7 percent women, compared with 10 percent for the FTSE 100 as a whole.

Membership of your executive committee should be one of your interim targets, because if you get there, your chances of making it to the board as an executive director of your company will clearly increase significantly. And executive committee membership is a valuable credential when you are seeking an appointment at another company as a NED. That is why female representation on the executive committee should be taken into account in target selection.

As we noted in Chapter 1, *The Female FTSE Report 2007* showed a sharp increase in the percentage of women on FTSE 100 executive committees from under 12 percent in 2006, to over 16 percent in 2007. It seems reasonable to assume that companies with relatively high percentages of women on their executive committees – Lloyds TSB and Shire, with more than 44 percent, and WPP, Home Retail Group, Next, Royal & Sun Alliance, Rentokil, Imperial Tobacco and Liberty International, with 25 percent or more – have less formidable labyrinths (see Chapter 4) for women than average and that their boards will be more accessible to women than average.

Setting milestones

Having chosen your preferred industries and preferred companies within them, and having assessed the accessibility of their boards to women, you should ask yourself what you need to do to be a strong candidate for their boards.

You have your target now, albeit provisional. You're ready to change your target, if opportunities present themselves outside your target zone, but you have a particular board, or a shortlist of boards, to aim for in the meantime.

Let us suppose your target is to be appointed a NED on the board of XYZ plc within five years. That is your personal strategic goal. Now you need to draw up a provisional list of personal projects, actions and achievements that will be required for you to reach that goal within the allotted five-year period. Working back from your goal, for example, you may conclude that you need to land your first board-like role (a school governor or local magistrate, perhaps) within 18 months, your first real board position (with a charity maybe or a National Health Service (NHS) Trust) within two-and-a-half years and your first corporate board (of an unlisted, or small listed company) within three years. Depending on your current circumstances, another set of milestones might include an appointment to a subsidiary board or your company's executive committee.

We will look at how to go about this credential-gathering in Chapter 9. The point here is that a strategic goal should be supported by a set of milestones or tactical goals that must be pursued right away, as soon as your strategic goal is set. Don't be too fussy with these interim goals. You can be fussier once you've passed a milestone or two. And always keep your options open. Tactical goals shouldn't be constraints either. Don't let them clutter up your vision or obscure your strategic goal. Grasp opportunities that seem consistent with your strategic goal when they come along, even if they are not quite what you had in mind when setting your interim goals.

Reflections for companies

In the war for talent, companies will gain an edge over their rivals when they make themselves more interesting for able women with board ambitions. It is possible that Cynthia Carroll's appointment as CEO of Anglo American in 2006 has made Anglo American in particular, and mining companies in general, considerably more attractive employers for ambitious women than they have been in the past. Companies at or near the

© Barbara Shore

top of the rankings for female representation on boards and executive committees are also transmitting welcome messages to women selecting targets for their board ambitions.

Companies can further expand their female catchment areas by widening their criteria for selecting board candidates. For example, they can remove from the criteria any formal or informal prejudices that may exist against women from pink collar functions, such as human resources (HR).

In their book *Managing Knowhow*, Karl-Erik Sveiby and Tom Lloyd argued that the de facto HR director in a "people business," or a "know-how company" was the CEO, because attracting and keeping good people was so close to the irreducible essence of the management challenge in this kind of business that it couldn't, or at any rate shouldn't, be delegated to a specialist function.[2]

Their definition of HR, that it was the front line in the "war for talent," wasn't the standard definition at the time. The conventional view was that HR was just "personnel with a college education," as Mark Twain might have said. It was seen as a largely administrative function, the role of which was to ensure the organization complied with employment laws and regulations, and that the terms of its formal contracts with employees were honored.

HR retains this administrative function today, but as more and more businesses have come to resemble people businesses, and the focus of attention has shifted from the formal contract to what Chris Argyris called the "psychological contract"[3] between employer and employees, HR has acquired a strategic (high-level, close to board) role, similar to the one Sveiby and Lloyd assigned to it in people businesses.

We believe that the prejudice against the HR function as a source of main board directors, evident in the scarcity of ex-HR executives on main boards and illustrated by the pejorative characterization of HR as a pink collar, far from the front line, function, reflects a general failure to recognize the change in HR's role in recent years, and is thus out of date.

According to Geoff Armstrong, former main board director of Standard Chartered and, from 1992 to 2008, director-general of the Chartered Institute of Personnel and Development (CIPD):

> There is a vast pool of talent within the HR profession, [which, if tapped at board level] would bring a new dimension to the non-executive role and ensure that an organization's key driver of value – namely its people – is taken seriously at board level.[4]

The CIPD launched a website in 2005 to provide information about corporate governance and the role of NEDs for CIPD members.[5] (The site also lists members interested in becoming NEDs.)

We agree with Armstrong. If companies were more willing to see in HR a source of directors as potentially fruitful as any other function, they would acquire better skills-balanced, as well as better gender-balanced boards and, because HR would consequently become a route to the top, and tend to attract more able people, they would also end up with better HR functions. Modern HR professionals have experience in change management, organizational design and executive development, and, thanks partly to the work of Karl-Erik Sveiby[6] and others on the valuation of "intangible assets," many of them are also becoming more financially literate.

References

1. "The woman who shook the City," *Sunday Times*, October 26, 2006.
2. *Managing Knowhow*, Karl-Erik Sveiby and Tom Lloyd, Bloomsbury, 1987.
3. *Understanding Organizational Behaviour*, Chris Argyris, Dorsey Press, 1960.
4. "Missing out," *People Management*, August 9, 2007.
5. www.cipd.co.uk/nedresource/information/corpgov.htm.
6. *The New Organizational Wealth: Managing and Measuring Knowledge-based Assets*, Karl-Erik Sveiby, Berrett-Koehler, 1997.

CHAPTER 6

Cultivating board qualities

Don't be such a slave to objectives that you forget to be true to yourself.

Sir Richard Evans, chairman, United Utilities plc

Who is this person who has the temerity to believe she has something worthwhile to contribute to a main board? Is she really you now, or someone you believe you can become in the future? If she is not you as you are now, how does she differ, and in what ways would you have to change to become her?

Whether or not you have been conscious of doing so, you have adapted yourself to every new position, role and set of circumstances you've reached, been assigned and found yourself in. We all do it. It's how we grow, develop and explore our potential. New jobs, challenges and circumstances invoke aspects of ourselves that might otherwise have remained latent, and bring out talents and aptitudes we might not previously have suspected that we possessed. Life is the chisel that sculpts us all – the nurturing that triggers the expressions of our nature that comprise our personalities.

Successful people prepare themselves for advancement by anticipating the nurture that will shape them the next level up. They try to show to those in whose gifts their promotions lie that they're qualified; they have what it will take; they're overqualified for or underused in their current roles, and are ready for new challenges. It's the same with main board positions. People who aspire to them should begin to cultivate and project main board qualities beforehand.

The difficulty for women, as they survey the board milieu at the top of the T-piece, is that being male seems to be one of the qualities associated with main boards and it is hard for them to cultivate and project that quality while remaining true to themselves.

Self-creation

On August 24, 1847, Mr. Currer Bell sent the manuscript of a novel to publisher Smith, Elder and Co. in London. In a note accompanying the MS, which had already been rejected by five publishers, Mr. Bell apologized for not prepaying the carriage (the local post office in Bradford could not accept money) and asked the publisher to address its correspondence "under cover to Miss Bronte, Haworth, Bradford, Yorkshire," because there was "a risk of letters otherwise directed not reaching me at present." The novel was *Jane Eyre*. Currer Bell was the pseudonym of Charlotte Bronte (1816–55), which she had assumed because the literary establishment of the day, including such figures as William Wordsworth and poet laureate Robert Southey, had made it clear that novel-writing was not a proper pastime for a lady.

Marian Evans said she wrote under the pen name George Eliot (1819–80), because she wanted her gritty psychological novels set in provincial England to be taken seriously, rather than dismissed as mere romances of the kind usually associated with female authors of the day. She may also have wished to shield her complicated and, by Victorian standards, scandalous private life, including her relationship with the married George Henry Lewes, from the glare of public scrutiny. And her male pen name was an effective cover for her role as assistant editor and de facto editor of the campaigning left-wing journal *The Westminster Review*. Women writers were not uncommon at the time, but it was very unusual, not to say unheard of, for a young, unmarried woman to lead a campaigning journal and move freely in London's predominantly male literary society.

Another female George was the French novelist and feminist, Amantine Aurore Lucile Dupin, Baronne Dudevant, alias George Sand (1804–76). It's clear from her journals and letters that Sand had no wish to be a man. Her trousers and pipe were just her tickets to the intellectual life of Paris. For Sand to have remained Baronne Dudevant, in appearance and style as well as in fact, would have been to deny her true self. The Sand persona was an adaptation to a society that denied higher class French women the mental stimulation many yearned for.

Although less studied and theatrical than George Sand, the Currer Bell and George Eliot personae were also adaptations to prevailing social norms that constrained or impeded their creators in some way. All these masquerades were successful, because, by disguising the gender of their creators, they allowed the development of what were, in the contexts in which the personae were deployed, more important aspects of their creators' personalities.

There is less need for gender deceptions these days, because being a woman is less of a disadvantage – isn't it? Joanne (Jo) Rowling has no middle name, but she was persuaded by her publisher, Bloomsbury, to adopt one (she chose her paternal grandmother's name, Kathleen) and only to use her initials as author of her Harry Potter books. Bloomsbury argued that her main target readers were young boys, and they would be more attracted to books about magic written by a man, rather than by a woman.

We adopt different personae in different situations and in different company. We're *mother* and *partner* at home, *daughter* with our parents and *colleague* and *manager* at work. We're *friend* with our friends and *customer* when shopping. Our personalities are portfolios of personae we don and discard to suit our situation. All of them are, or should be, authentic expressions of our personalities.

But when choosing from your portfolios of personae one that seems to suit the current setting, you flout the constraints imposed by your gender and the social norms at your peril. People, usually men, will decide whether or not you are appointed to a board. One male client told us that he disliked what he saw as the "masculine" persona of a woman on a board he served on. "We don't want someone playing a part on our board. We want genuine people, at ease with themselves." So change your persona to suit the circumstances by all means, but when you do, understand the circumstances and the audiences to which your chosen personae will be playing.

Sir Richard Evans, chairman of United Utilities plc, and a mentor on the FTSE 100 Cross-Company Mentoring Programme, made the same point in a different way:

> The other ingredient that's hugely important is chemistry. You just have to accept that sometimes the chemistry in a relationship doesn't "click." It's not an indictment of the person's ability. There must be a chemistry fit within a team – if two people [on a team] don't have it, it can affect the whole team. You have to make a judgment. It's not to do with people's competency – you can't train people at this level to create the right chemistry.

> Personality is part of chemistry. Don't think so much about getting boxes ticked that you forget your natural behavior. It's true that for women to distinguish themselves, they have to put more effort in than men, but don't be such a slave to objectives that you forget to be true to yourself.

Acting authentically

The heading of this section seems like an oxymoron. When you act, you play a part, by definition, and if you are playing a part, you can't be authentic. How can you always be authentic – always your own self – if, as we're suggesting, you assume different roles with different people, in different situations? It's a good question, and one we've struggled with ourselves.

Our answer is that the apparent paradox is resolved if you think of personae, rather than parts or roles. We are not suggesting you play different parts in different situations. We're suggesting you deploy different aspects of your true self in different situations.

The acting comes in because you are more practiced at deploying some of your personae than others. You don't have to think any more about how to be a friend, because your friend persona is hardwired in your tacit memory. Deploying it is automatic, like driving a car. But you do have to think about being a wife or a partner in the early stages of a relationship, and about being a mother when your first child is born. A friend of ours remembers being taken aback momentarily when she was told by the maternity nurse that she had to feed her newborn son. It didn't seem fair. She was exhausted after a long and painful labor. All she wanted to do was sleep. Her mother persona was also newborn. She hadn't acquired the habits and reflexes that would soon hardwire "mother" into her subconscious. She had to "act" mother in the meantime, consciously.

It's the same with your board persona. It is authentically you right from the start, in that it incorporates your values and beliefs, but you have to act your way into it, until your "director" persona is established and deploys itself automatically. As it assembles itself from bits and pieces of other, more familiar personae, you will need consciously to invent (the word comes from the Latin for find) new aspects of your personality that none of your existing personae have needed.

This is what we mean by acting authentically. When you're integrating a new persona, for a new situation, such as being on your first main board, you will always have to act, to some extent, in a deliberate and conscious way. It will become automatic later.

The first requirement in developing and deploying a persona is being self-aware – being aware of yourself as an actor and taking control of your appearance and emotions. The second is to ensure that the persona you are developing is fit for purpose.

You might like to consider treating high-level meetings, attended by those whom it is in your long-term interests to impress, as a kind of theatre and employ theatrical methods. "All the world's a stage, and all the men and women merely players," as Shakespeare said in *As you Like It*. Keep your audience guessing by allowing your view to emerge slowly. Don't put all your cards on the table right away. Timing is of the essence. Think about how you can heighten the dramatic effect of your contributions and control, or exert influence, on the pattern and tempo of the meeting. It goes without saying that to orchestrate proceedings in this way, you need some sort of agenda or intention; something to say. That is why preparation is vital. On the basis of what you know of the meeting agenda and the views of others, run through possible dialogue scenarios in your mind beforehand. Try to anticipate and prepare responses to possible questions and counterarguments. Use silence to create tension when appropriate and humor to defuse it.

Remember that each meeting is one encounter in a series and that you have strategic, as well as tactical objectives. Winning the argument in one meeting should never compromise your chance of getting on the board, or a board. The personae you assume and the ways you use them need to carry you successfully well beyond the meeting. They must be consistent as well as adaptable, likeable as well as tough, easy to be with as well as challenging and compatible, in personal chemistry terms, as well as distinctive.

In short, those who encounter your board candidate persona in formal and informal settings should begin to feel about you as Mark Antony felt about Brutus; "the elements so mixed in [her]" that she is a cert for a board appointment sometime soon.

Let us now look in more detail at one of the qualities people expect in a main board director, which many women and quite a few men often struggle to acquire.

The weighty question of gravitas

The word gravitas comes from the Latin *gravis* meaning heavy, serious. It is defined in the Oxford English Dictionary as "dignity or solemnity of manner", as in: "a frivolous biography that lacks the gravitas of its subject." Gravitas is usually associated with qualities such as experience, authority, seriousness, wisdom and calm self-confidence. Because of its association with experience, and having "seen it all before," gravitas in the general sense is more often found in older people. But younger people can be seen to have gravitas when talking of matters or on subjects they're intimate with, or issues they have clearly thought deeply about.[1]

It's a relative thing. The same person can come across as having the quality of gravitas in one setting or on one subject, but seem to be lightweight, which is an antonym of gravitas, in another setting or on another subject. Gravitas is slow and considered, not quick or clever. It employs dry humor and irony, but not frivolity, jokiness or chattiness. Its language is conservative and sparing. Those who possess the quality of gravitas talk less than others, but what they say carries more weight, by definition.

The reason gravitas is so important and why we tell clients never to run or scuttle (gravitas never scuttles) into meetings three minutes before the start, and to "wait for the second beat" before responding is because what you are doing on a board and elsewhere is *exercising your judgment*. If you do things on the run, if you're always late and in a hurry, if you speak off the cuff before you've had a moment to think, people are likely to entertain doubts about the quality of your judgment. So arrive at meetings in good time so you don't seem flustered (gravitas is never flustered), think more before you speak and speak in a measured way as far as you can. Reflect, consider and constantly hone your judgment. Your goal, on a board, is to convince your fellow directors to respect your opinions, give them reasons to value your counsel, and persuade them to act on your recommendations.[2]

Gravitas is one of the qualities that are hard to define, but easily recognized. It's seldom immediately apparent, however. A low-pitched male voice may create the expectation of gravitas, but the authentic quality is built up cumulatively, and more by words, arguments and demeanor, than pitch of voice. The impression of gravitas emerges. It's probably harder for women, with their higher pitched voices, to predispose people to expect it, but, unlike leadership qualities, it is not associated exclusively with male traits.

Anyone who reaches the board milieu and becomes a credible candidate for a board appointment will have already acquired a certain amount of gravitas in the eyes of people lower down the organization. So it is partly a matter of bringing the demeanor and style that created that perception with you to the board milieu, and resisting your own tendency to revert to, and sometimes the efforts of others to impose on you, a "newbie" or ingénue role in the higher powered company you will be keeping.

You can use various strategies to increase your gravitas, based on a thoughtful analysis of the meaning of the word and the components of which it seems to you to consist. For instance, you can try to model your behavior on that of those within and outside your organization whom you and others perceive as possessing gravitas or one or more of its components. Or you can derive, from your analysis of the word's meaning, a few simple behavioral rules and school yourself to abide by them.

One client used the qualities that Rudyard Kipling lists in his poem "If" as his gravitas model. He learned the poem by heart and would recite lines to himself that seemed relevant to his situation at the time.

Another used the mantra: "I *will* act as a statesman." He repeated it to himself in meetings before opening his mouth. It was a successful strategy. Before he derived his mantra from his analysis of the idea of gravitas, he was widely regarded as overemotional, superficial and somewhat unpredictable. Three years later he was regarded as the most statesman-like director on the board.

Gravitas is an important quality for a director, but you're not born either with or without it. It is a quality that can be deliberately cultivated. If you assume a calm, considered persona and diligently school yourself always to behave in a way that projects gravitas, you will come to be seen as having gravitas.

Raising your profile

Your objective, when cultivating an impression of gravitas and other board qualities, is to create a particular kind of image of yourself in the minds of others, which will say "board material" to those who are making decisions. This is what you take to market in the board milieu. It's the persona you use in informal sounding-outs, formal interviews and presentations.

But it's not enough to create the right image. You must also sell it, and many women find this quite difficult. Selling yourself smacks of ambition and they're uncomfortable with ambition, because they think it implies ruthlessness. As a consequence, they are less inclined to push themselves forward than men and are, therefore, often perceived to be less ambitious. This is a problem, because ambition is also a board quality. "She's got to want to get there," one of our mentors said of his mentee. "It's a waste of time otherwise." Because of the preponderance of male directors, the board milieu, and the places and events where board candidates socialize, is alive with ambition. Women must find ways to compete effectively in the board milieu and be seen to "want to get there." If you dislike words like "ambition" and "goals," use words such as "aspiration" and "realizing my potential" instead.

And you really must get out more. For all sorts of valid reasons, women often confine themselves to the tasks they are accountable for and keep low profiles elsewhere. They must deploy their candidate personae outside their comfort zones, if they harbor board ambitions. They should attend conferences and go to meetings on more general strategic issues; be opinionated, well informed and vocal; take a few calculated risks; make sure those who matter know what they've achieved already and that they're eager for new challenges.

Authentic, impressive and memorable personalities are appointed to main boards, not those masquerading as their conceptions of an ideal (ergo, male) director, who are hard work socially, one dimensional or passive. Board candidates must put themselves about a bit, raise their profiles above their local parapets, make an impression on and earn the respect of others, while remaining true to themselves, and their values and beliefs. If you really want to get there, you must take up residence in "candidate space"; become visible; project your board qualities at every appropriate opportunity; act the part and generally make it easy for headhunters and their clients to put you on (and hard to leave you off) shortlists for board appointments.

Credibility is the key, and to be credible you must appear to others to be at ease with yourself when doing these things and behaving in these ways. You need to "grow yourself up," as we say, and hardwire your chosen candidate persona as an aspect of the real you.

Looking the part

Profile, image and gravitas can be conveyed on paper with your power CV, by your behavior, by profile-raising and last, but by no means least, by your appearance. Looking the part is vital for a would-be director, because, as the saying goes, "you never get a second chance to make a first impression."

Just as feedback is helpful when developing your leadership style, it should also play a part in testing and corroborating your appearance and how you present yourself. Asking for comments on your appearance is not easy, because the way we habitually dress, apply makeup and present ourselves goes to the very core of how we perceive ourselves in the world, but it can be of tremendous benefit. If you receive and take good advice, you will know you are looking good and your self-confidence will get a boost.

As you move up from the vertical into the horizontal element of the T-piece, you should put away high-street tailoring and styles, and cultivate a more individual and sophisticated image. To work out the right professional look for you, note what other senior women in the organization wear, and decide on which, often subtle, shifts you need to make to look more the board-level executive. Company dress codes may not be very helpful for women, because they're often rudimentary and mostly for men, and there may not be any female role models. But they usually contain some clues.

Don't be afraid to get advice from professional style consultants on colors, styles and so on, and buy the best quality clothes you feel you can afford. You don't need a whole new wardrobe; quality is more important than quantity here. A major dilemma for most professional women is how to appear businesslike and feminine, at the same time. We have thankfully moved on from the power dressing of the 1980s and there is no longer a need to wear a man's suit, which can look too severe and masculine, but you should avoid styles that could be seen as provocative, or indiscreet. It is also important to look current, without being a slave to fashion. Regular updating of your wardrobe to keep it looking fresh will help.

Finally, pay attention to hair, nails and skin (they say a lot about you), do all you can to stay fit and healthy and ensure that you get enough sleep (if you look tired all the time, you may look as if you can't cope) and take regular exercise.

Reflections for companies

Left to their own devices, male-dominated corporate cultures tend to "freeze out," as Winston Churchill put it (see Chapter 2), opinionated and vocal women, or, at any rate, make it difficult for women to be opinionated and vocal, and still be seen as feminine. By according such women respect and admiration, company leaders can help level the playing field. As the arbiters of credibility, companies with board vacancies should carefully and objectively review their official and unofficial criteria for judging credibility, to ensure those criteria are free of hidden prejudices and inappropriate, or outdated assumptions.

They should also try to remove from their board candidate space male qualities, such as macho language and the focus on sport, so that women do not feel, and are not in fact, excluded from the networking and social dimensions of the candidate space.

As always in this kind of culture change program, little is likely to happen without strong leadership from the top. The following case study is exemplary in this respect.

Improving women retention at JPMorgan

In early 2007, management at JPMorgan, the investment bank, decided to take decisive steps to improve the recruitment and retention of women and in particular to address the relatively low percentage of women reaching managing director level in the front office. While women make up over a third of employees at the analyst level, this proportion drops as the population becomes more senior. In common with other firms, JPMorgan's management wanted to differentiate itself and improve the overall percentage of women at the more senior levels of the investment bank.

The bank was already undertaking a number of initiatives in this area and had been recognized for its work in The Times Top 50 Firms Where Women Want to Work, but the number of women at senior level was not improving. As part of a range of initiatives designed to attract and retain female employees, Klaus Diederichs, the head of investment banking coverage in Europe, decided to lead a program of work aimed at ensuring that responsibility for female retention lay firmly on the shoulders of the bank's senior managers. Research undertaken by JPMorgan into the reasons women gave for leaving the bank had pointed to the importance of the role of the manager in providing opportunities for women to develop their careers, and in creating a climate where they felt valued and supported.

To make it clear that he believed that change could only take place if senior managers themselves took this issue seriously, Diederichs proposed that managers' performance in the area of female retention should be assessed as part of their annual appraisal and reflected in their annual bonuses. This was agreed by the Co-CEO of the investment bank, Bill Winters. In addition, to help them be successful, he decided personally to invite every MD in the investment bank in Europe to attend sessions aimed at making them aware of the bank's performance in female retention; to share their experiences, perspectives and best practice in managing and retaining women; and to give them tools and guidance on how to provide a working environment where women could develop their careers successfully. Some 80 percent of the bank's managing director population has now been through the workshops, each of which was led by a senior management colleague and co-facilitated by one of the authors of this book, and her colleague.

At the time of writing (January 2008), it is too early to assess the long-term impact of this initiative, but it is clear that it has raised the profile of the issue across the bank, helped leaders to recognize their role and provided them with invaluable guidance ... and they were all talking about it!

References

1. *Gravitas*, John Coleman, Christopher Cooper, Robin Linnecar et al., Praesta, 2007.
2. "Being on a board," Peninah Thomson, in Mirella Visser and Annalisa Gigante (eds) *Women on Boards: Moving Mountains*, EuropeanPNW in association with Mercer, EPWN Women@WorkNo.8.

CHAPTER 7

Setting out your stall

Generally, board directors "elect themselves." It's obvious to their peers and to others. They rise to the top, acquire a track record of performance and demonstrate personal and business values.

David Reid, chairman, Tesco plc

The English intellectual Thomas de Quincey (1785–1859), friend of Wordsworth and Coleridge and best known for his *Confessions of an English Opium Eater* (1822), made a distinction between the literature of knowledge and the literature of power:

> The function of the first is – to *teach*; the function of the second is – to *move*: the first is a rudder, the second an oar or a sail.[1]

CVs seldom have any literary pretensions, but if yours had to be categorized in de Quincy's terms, would you say it was an example of the literature of knowledge, or the literature of power? It may seem to be an example of the literature of knowledge, because its function is surely to *teach* those who read it about you and what you've achieved. But it is actually, or at any rate, should be, an example of the literature of power, because its real function is to *move* those who see it to put you on the list of applicants for the job who seem worth interviewing.

Heard the one about the Nomco chairman who split his unread CVs into two piles and binned one of the piles, on the grounds that he didn't want unlucky people on his board? It is seldom as arbitrary as that, of course, but you should think hard about what you say in your CV, how you say it, and the criteria those who will read it are likely to use, when dividing the CV pile in two. Your CV *must* get on the right pile, because those on the other pile are destined for the bin.

There's much more to getting appointed to a board than a powerful CV of course, but a document that can get you through initial screening processes, when the competition is purely documentary, should not be taken lightly.

This chapter is about marketing yourself effectively. We shall begin with the CV, which is in a sense the end result of the process, and work back through targets to plans. It makes sense doing it this way for two reasons – first, because CV competition is usually the first round in a board selection tournament, and if you don't get through the first round, little else matters; second, because the process of developing a "power CV" will clarify your mind about yourself, as a board candidate, and help you to decide what strengths and successes to emphasize, and generally how to brand and position yourself. What you learn, in this process, will be useful later, for example when preparing for interviews and presentations to particular groups.

Try to get some help when drafting your CV. With wise and perceptive company on your journey of self-discovery, you're likely to discover more than you would on your own. Sir Mark Moody-Stuart, chairman of Anglo American, said:

> As a mentor, it was fascinating to help my mentee bring out her own skills and background: to identify with her the breadth of her skills, beyond the usual summary of professional capabilities that's the basis of a job application. Together, we recast her CV in a way that would be of interest to a chairman looking for a non-executive director.

In addition to being a key marketing document in its own right, your CV is the basic template of your whole personal marketing program. It will help to set the agenda for discussions in the interviews it will lead to (if it is powerful enough) and you can seed it with openings for the prepared "stories" you want to tell, of which more later.

Developing a power CV

A power CV is multifunctional. First, it handles all the stuff that makes a CV seem part of the "literature of knowledge" (schooling, academic and professional qualifications, positions held, and so on) and, crucially, it also provides the impetus that moves it onto the right list. It should include three kinds of information:

- *Qualifiers:* academic and professional qualifications, and the skills and experience you need just to be a contender.

- *Differentiators:* your own personal selling points; the particular talents, skills, abilities and experiences that you feel will favorably differentiate you from other candidates.

- *Personality markers:* information about your interests, values and beliefs, which will allow the reader to form a provisional view of your personality, and of how compatible you are likely to be with those with whom you will be working.

An example of a CV of this kind is set out below. It won't look like this to the reader, because you should see your CV as a master document from which to select particular sets of components to suit the circumstances. The same goes for presentations and preparations for interviews. We have found, while working with women applying for new jobs, that it sometimes comes as a surprise to them to find they have, in effect, to rewrite their CVs for each application. Using the same CV every time is asking for it to be binned.

You must be succinct and efficient in your personal marketing. Apply Occam's razor (14th-century English logician, William of Occam, said that explanations should make as few assumptions as possible). Only provide information relevant to those to whom you're presenting. The qualities of economy and efficiency are, themselves, admirable. Your marketing should demonstrate them.

Example of a power CV

Joanna Templeton BSc FCA

Address:	Downside Farm	Telephone:	12345 6789 (home)
	Commonside, Bucks		9876 54321 (mobile)
	AB1 XY9	Email:	templeton.j@xxxxxxx.com

PERSONAL PROFILE

A commercially astute and energetic leader with a proven track record of financial restructuring, flotations and M&A work gained in both line and functional roles. With good communication, motivation and presentation skills, has demonstrated a real ability to achieve corporate objectives in operational and program environments. Respected for strong influencing skills, drive and tenacity combined with sound commercial insight and excellent analytical capabilities.

PROFESSIONAL EXPERIENCE AND ACHIEVEMENTS

2004–present ILLUSORY HOLDINGS plc: property and leisure group – market capitalization £300m, employees 1,000 direct, with 10,000 franchisees.

Finance Director, Property Division, comprising 2,000 properties in England and Wales which produce a profit of £25m before tax. Responsible for financial management and accounting for the division, monitoring weekly cash flow, preparation of

---

monthly management reports, annual budgets, quarterly rolling forecasts and variance analysis. Also responsible for the group's car fleet. Staff of 25. Main achievements:

- Improved management effectiveness by developing a new computerized management reporting system and a detailed client database.

- Focused attention on profitability by installing a performance-linked bonus scheme for field staff, credit controller and tenants.

- Improved cash flow by instituting financial controls generally and with particular emphasis on cash collection, consumables and refurbishment costs.

- Introduced a bimonthly newsletter, dramatically improving communication with tenants.

Director of Corporate Finance, reporting to the chairman and responsible for the critical group treasury function, monitoring cash flow, liaison with the group's bankers and professional advisers, supervising the preparation and subsequent analysis of the strategic plans for existing businesses, identifying potential acquisitions and disposals. Main achievements:

- Contributed to the recent successful restructuring and subsequent relisting of the group.

- Negotiated and completed two Eurobond issues each worth 500m euros.

- Managed the financial and legal aspects of 10 major acquisitions.

- Evaluated numerous corporate financing schemes, including long-term debenture issues, deep discount bonds and sale and leaseback schemes.

1998–2004 TOUCHE MARWICK: one of the largest international accountancy and consulting partnerships. Following articles and achievement of professional qualifications, progressed from **Trainee Accountant** to **Senior Manager** and gained experience of corporate finance and audit work, managing other professionals, acquisition investigations, the preparation of accountants' reports and listing particulars for companies seeking membership of the London Stock Exchange and investigations in support of litigation.

EDUCATIONAL AND PROFESSIONAL QUALIFICATIONS

19XX–XX **XYZ School**, Leicestershire: 10 O levels; 3 A levels (Economics, Maths, Geography).

19XX–XX **XYZ University:** First Class BSc (Hons) in Economics with Accountancy.

19XX **Fellow of Institute of Chartered Accountants in England & Wales (FCA):** Qualified first attempt.

19XX **XYZ University**, Integrated Management Program.

INTERESTS/OTHER

Married with two children, Caroline and James.

I enjoy leisure travel, fund-raising for XYZ Charity, hill-walking and socializing with friends.

Adapting to circumstances

When selling yourself through a CV, presentation or interview at a one-off event, or a series of encounters, to strangers, or to people who already know you well, you need to present yourself in the best possible light, given the circumstances. To do that you need to have a good understanding of those circumstances and of the people and organizations to whom and to which you're selling yourself.

Think about the organization's current needs and culture, and, given those needs and that culture, try to work out what and whom those who are doing the appointing will be looking for. Think hard also about the demands of the director role you are aiming for, the experience and skills it appears to require and how closely your own experience and skills match those requirements. You should then work out how to demonstrate in convincing ways that you have the required experience and skills, how to suggest that the personal chemistry is compatible, and generally how to persuade your interviewers that there are "good fits" between you and the role, and you and the organization.

You may find it helpful to be systematic about this; to list all the perceived requirements and weight them according to what you suspect their importance is to each board or panel member. Don't reserve all the high weights for the qualifiers (see above); not even the most hard-headed and disciplined of selectors can be entirely objective. Sometimes a "nice to have" quality will seem so nice and fit so well that it will offset an inadequacy in a "must-have."

Baroness Hogg, chairman of 3i plc, advises board candidates to adapt to the circumstances and listen:

> A candidate's credibility depends primarily on what he or she is seen as bringing to the party – which is not just experience and expertise, though these are critical, but also the ability to engage, and interact effectively and positively. So, when discussing a possible board position, be on receive, rather than transmit: learn what the nominations committee feel the board lacks, how the board works, what the key issues are and also how the board tackles them. That will

help you to understand how you can help the board operate more effectively, which should mean more harmoniously, even when the issues are difficult or divisive ones ... But, of course, engagement is not enough in itself: if you don't have relevant experience and expertise to begin with, you will lack the credibility to engage effectively anyway.

The power of the tale

The best way to convey the points that you believe your selectors want to hear is to tell stories about your successes and achievements, and about deployments of your talents and skills. PAST (problem analysis solution triumph) is a helpful mnemonic. Using a logical sequence of this kind when shaping your stories will help you remember them, and tell them fluently and concisely. If you can, rehearse them out loud in front of friends, family members or a coach. A rehearsal audience doesn't need to be as familiar with the subject as those who will be interviewing you to judge the quality of your delivery. Or you could record your delivery in audio and video and act as your own critic.

Always end on a high note; a note of achievement. That's not as easy as it sounds in a stressful situation, where your interlocutors have the power to interrupt your delivery with questions and requests for clarifications. But keeping in mind the desirability of ending with a upbeat coda or culmination will help to give the tale the right shape and rhythm.

Life planning

Your power CV backed up with the prepared and rehearsed interview material that will be needed if your CV does its job and gets you on that "worth interviewing" list emerge from the targeting process we discussed in Chapter 5. They comprise a personal marketing strategy derived from a higher level career strategy. In other words, they're the product of a well-thought-out plan. And just as your overall targets are provisional, your personal marketing strategy must be a work in progress. You should revisit it regularly, as your career progresses, your milestones are achieved, and chance encounters, new interests and a wider network of colleagues and acquaintances create new possibilities you didn't anticipate when writing the first draft of your marketing strategy.

All the evidence points to the fact that those with a plan do better than those who let their lives unfold and react to the opportunities and problems that fortune throws at them.

Your provisional targets are part of the plan. They will help you to identify the list of opportunities at which your personal marketing strategy should be aimed. But there is much thinking to be done before you set your targets, because you don't want to aim too low.

In setting your sights, you can try using a procedure that a number of our clients have found helpful:

1.　Choose a goal you would love to achieve, but which you feel is beyond you, and which you are, therefore, currently making no attempt to reach.

2.　Do what we call a "possibility brainstorm"; spend five minutes thinking of as many ways as you can to bring it within reach.

3.　Make two plans: one going forwards from where you are now; the other going backwards from your "impossible" goal. If you can get them to meet in the middle, it may not be impossible after all.

4.　Find at least three pieces of evidence, no matter how small or apparently trivial, that your impossible dream is already in the process of being realized.

5.　Find three things that you can do right now that will increase the chances, even if only slightly, of reaching your goal.

6.　Each morning for a week repeat your possibility brainstorm for three minutes, each day take three actions, each evening write down three pieces of evidence.

7.　Wait for "the way" to emerge. You will know when it happens, because you will find yourself taking more and more actions towards what you want – you will have begun to live the impossible dream.[2]

Putting your head above the parapet

The days are long gone, in the UK anyway, when the roles of chairman and CEO were combined, and the *capo di tutti capi* (boss of bosses) was able to stuff his board with yes men (and, very occasionally, yes women) on whom he could rely to support his grand strategy without question, and act as lobby fodder during votes. Today, most chairmen are non-executive and most of those we know see themselves as sculptors and conductors of teams of all the talents. If vacancies arise on their boards, they seek personable, opinionated, self-confident men and women who seem to have good judgment and the strength of character to insist, demand and refuse, and generally to resist the seductions of "groupthink."

© Barbara Shore

SETTING OUT YOUR STALL

One of the main challenges for women who want to join main boards is thus to gain reputations for being personable, opinionated and self-confident, of being their own women, of having strong characters. In other words, as they approach the board, they need to put their heads above the parapet; raise their profiles; have something to say; and be heard saying it. Speak at conferences. Get articles published in publications likely to be read by people by whom you may be interviewed. Pen an occasional punchy letter to the *Financial Times*, *Daily Telegraph* or *The Times*. Cultivate relationships with print and broadcast journalists and get on their lists of people who "know what they are talking about," who talk well about it and can be approached for a comment.

Lorraine Heggessey, the first woman appointed controller of BBC One and then in 2005 appointed CEO of talkbackTHAMES (one of the UK's largest production companies), who is one of the mentees on the FTSE 100 Cross-Company Mentoring Programme, has been mentioned in a number of articles and she had some trenchant, controversial things to say about the future of UK television when she was interviewed by the *Independent* in late 2007.[3]

No doubt some people who read that article profoundly disagreed with her, but whatever their own views on the subject, most readers were left with the impression that this woman was thoughtful, articulate and not only knew her stuff, but was a recognized authority on the subject.

Reflections for companies

Companies wishing to appoint more women to their boards also need to make plans and pursue them actively, because if they allow events to take their natural course, it may take them decades to eradicate hidden biases in their corporate cultures entirely and fill up their board candidate pipelines with more women.

We've already suggested ways to approach culture change in our first book, *A Woman's Place is in the Boardroom*, and in earlier chapters of this book. It is necessary, but it's not easy, or quick. Companies that want to take the lead in the war for talent in general, and boardroom gender-balancing in particular, should try to accelerate the culture change processes and take more deliberate steps to enrich their board candidate pipelines with more women.

Just as the causes of the pipeline problem – the paucity of women in the candidate space – are multifaceted, so too are its solutions. It is a jigsaw, in the sense that it consists of many pieces that must be fitted together into an integrated strategy. We discussed some of these pieces in Chapter 9, Priming the pipeline, in our first book. Since then, we've thought more deeply and worked more with companies endeavoring to attract, retain and develop executive-level female talent. On the basis of research conducted by the consultancy firm, Brook Graham, for *The Female FTSE Report 2005*,[4] which highlighted best practice in 12 FTSE 100 companies, and our ongoing work in this arena, we propose that companies should take action in five areas.

Set targets

To achieve an objective, such as women accounting for one-quarter of executive directors in a decade, a company will have to hit a set of inter-mediate targets, such as women accounting for 30 percent of the executives at two levels below the board within four years and women accounting for 20 percent of executives at one level below the board within six years. These intermediate goals could then be broken down into targets for each function, department and business unit and for each planning period year, and formally incorporated into the planning system or balanced scorecard. Once annual targets are set, plans can be drawn up to ensure that each part of the business actively pursues its own targets and so achieves its specified annual contribution to the group target.

Rise above the "noise"

Target-setting is always controversial. There's bound to be a lot of criticism, from women as well as men, of both targeting in principle and the specific targets set. Strong leadership is needed here. The chairman should give his or her support to the CEO and the executive committee in setting targets and then holding people accountable for achieving them. If a succession plan comes before the board with no women on the provisional shortlist, the chairman and the other NEDs should use the "power of the well-placed question."

We should emphasize strongly that we don't advocate *quotas* for women at particular management levels. Targets are different from quotas. They are used throughout organizations as a mechanism for conveying priorities and improving performance in all sorts of areas. A target gives businesses something to aim for and helps to measure year-on-year improvement, but does not replace competition on merit for roles.

Nurture talent

Don't allow your able women to opt for pink collar roles too early on in their careers. Try to identify them in good time and take steps to ensure that they are assigned to operational and expatriate roles that give them experience and visibility. As they approach the board, allow women and men in your executive talent pool to take NED positions in other companies and sectors. If their line managers say they can't spare them, or that it will distract them or dilute their focus on their current jobs, point out that such outside assignments will give them a more objective view of their jobs by widening their horizons, in addition to providing much-needed board experience.

Open the books

Be open, with shareholders and employees, about your gender-balanced pipeline program. Publish your long-term and intermediate targets, if you decide to set them, and your progress towards achieving them in, for instance, the diversity or corporate social responsibility (CSR) section of the annual report. If you choose not to set targets, publish your figures anyway. Annual measurement focuses attention on trends and prepares minds for action.

Review your criteria

Think carefully about the criteria you use when shortlisting people for senior positions, including board positions. As we have already seen, official criteria, such as a prejudice against promotions from certain functions, and unofficial criteria, such as the unconscious, but common assumption that leadership qualities are most often found in men, clog up pipelines and labyrinths (see Chapter 4) with obstacles that select against women in the competition for high office.

In their booklet, *Building a New Board: Lessons from Spinoffs*, headhunters Spencer Stuart liken the assembly of a board to filling in a bingo card. Each square of the bingo card represents one must-have skill, experience, or quality.[5] Board architects (a business unit spun off from a large group often needs to build its board more or less from scratch) see diversity in age, gender, race, ethnicity and geographic location as a desirable, underlying quality of the whole bingo card, rather than a box in its own right. According to Spencer Stuart, boards aren't seeking diversity to be politically correct or because of outside pressures, "but because it expands their views on issues, options and solutions." Looked at this way, women represent a bargain for board architects. They offer "two for the price of one," because in addition to filling in a must-have box, such as general board experience, board committee experience or particular expertise in marketing, they can also add to overall diversity, assuming, as is usually the case, most of the other boxes are ticked by men.

While on the subject of overall diversity, it is worth noting that a criticism often levelled at female talent management strategies is that they are largely designed with white women in mind. The numbers of black, minority, ethnic (BME) women at board level in the UK, and of women of color in the US, remain tiny, despite recent research published in the UK[6] suggesting that BME women bring the valuable addition to companies of "bicultural competence, being familiar with both British values and the norms of their ethnic groups." This, the report's authors suggest, gives them "the ability to manage and lead across cultures," which is "highly valuable in today's increasingly globalised business environment."

BME men also bring that quality of course, but the report argues that the

cultural breadth and learning, from the challenges and experiences … [BME women] have faced because of their race *and* gender, also give them the ability to see things from multiple perspectives and thus often come up with novel solutions to problems.

In her foreword to the report, Baroness Amos (EU special representative to the African Union and former leader of the House of Lords) said this overlay of gender and ethnic differences means

BME women come to the workplace with a knowledge of and commitment to British values, an understanding of the challenges facing their communities and experience gained from a range of sectors, including the voluntary sector and faith-based organisations. This helps to instil a values-driven approach to tackling organisational problems.

Companies that wish to benefit from such a bicultural competence at board level might reflect for a moment on the type of career support they offer to BME women in the corporate talent pipeline. The impact of the "double difference" of race *and* gender on career progression is made clear in the UK report and is well documented in the US. One should not assume that career experiences, obstacles and strategies are common to BME and white women. A company that employs a slightly differentiated approach to career management that accommodates these differences might be rewarded with slightly better results.

References

1. "The poetry of Pope," *North British Review*, August 1848.
2. *Constructing your CV*, John Coleman, Christopher Cooper, Robin Linnecar et al., Praesta, 2007.
3. "Lorraine Heggessey, still searching for the x factor," the *Independent*, November 8, 2007.
4. "Managing the female talent pipeline," in Lesley Brook and Jacey Graham, *The Female FTSE Report 2005*, Cranfield University School of Management.
5. *Cornerstone of the Board: Building a New Board – Lessons from Spinoffs*, Julie Hembrock Daum and Julie Cohen Norris, Spencer Stuart, 2007.
6. *Different Women, Different Places*, the Diversity Practice Ltd. and Katalytik Ltd., 2007, sponsored by Credit Suisse, Booz Allen Hamilton, Pearson, Learning & Skills Council, EU European Social Fund, UK Resource Centre for Women in Science, Engineering & Technology, Brown-Forman.

CHAPTER 8

Mind the gap

You must go through a self-assessment process. What can you "bring to the party" and, having gone to the party, how can you contribute? When you go onto a board for the first time, you have to think hard about whether, and how, you should intervene, and how you demonstrate your authority. The emphasis should be on quality, rather than frequency.

Roger Carr, chairman, Centrica plc

In the previous chapter, we discussed how to assemble your experience, aptitudes, skills and qualities into a credible persona for an executive or a non-executive board role and then promote it. Maybe you felt, while reading it, "that's all very well, but it's easier said than done" or "there must be more to it than developing a CV, raising my profile and planning my career." If so, you were quite right, of course. In our experience, that process, which sounds straightforward enough, often triggers or requires another, far more fundamental process that amounts to a root and branch self-examination.

Socrates said, "The unexamined life is not worth living."[1] The process of reviewing your experience, summarizing your track record to date and, having done so, identifying the sectors and companies that will suit you, and you them, is a valuable exercise in its own right, whatever conclusions you come to. It is valuable, too, because it will oblige you to take a closer look than you might have envisaged at who you are, what options are open to you, and where you are going with your professional (and sometimes also your personal) life.

This book is based on the concept of a roadmap, a reliable guide to help you on your journey towards a main board appointment. But what happens if you come to a roadblock? What happens if, while setting out your stall as we prescribe in the previous chapter, you realize that what promised beforehand to be a simple process of mapping out a logical progression, from where you have come from, through where you are now and on to where you want to be, reveals a complex, fractured, inconsistent and incomplete picture? In this chapter, we focus on what to do when you discover gaps that you will somehow have to bridge between where and who you are now, and where and who you would like to be.

Busy, busy

First, it's worth noting that many senior executives, men and women (including yourself, perhaps), never actually get round to asking themselves if there is any disparity between how they *are* leading their professional lives and how they would *like* to lead them. The "faster, faster," as Heather Dawson put it,[2] "busy, busy" nature of working life leaves most of us with very little time to reflect. It is often easier just to keep going – to rush from one thing to another, from one role to the next, without really stopping to make sure the destination to which we are rushing is really the place we want to arrive at.

This is risky, for two reasons. First, because we may end up with a life quite unlike the one we would have wished for. Second, because if we are not careful, we may, while simply keeping going, repeat mistakes and patterns of mistakes we've made in the past, which lead inevitably to more stress and possibly even trigger burnout.[3]

We will assume in this chapter, however, that these risks have been recognized, and will have in mind the woman who *is* taking the time to reflect upon what she wants to do with her life and in what kind of situation, industry and company she wants to make a contribution as an experienced executive.

Reflect before you leap

The decision to engage and "go for it" does confront you, in a real sense, with a gap. It may not seem very wide, in that the far side may not seem very different from the side you're on, but if you try to leap it, without carefully inspecting the gap itself and your own leaping abilities, there are two potential downsides. First, you may not succeed in leaping, because you haven't done that homework, and you may, therefore, have to step hurriedly back to safe ground and start all over again. Second, and even worse, you may get stuck in a seemingly inescapable cycle of leaping and failing, repeating a pattern of mistakes that destroys working relationships and leads to eventual disillusionment.

Female executives who want to fulfil their potential must recognize that the process of reflection, of developing deep personal insight and awareness, is valuable in and of itself for their own good, and is also a vital step in the development of their ability to "read" others, to understand the social dynamics at every level, including board level, and to engage in them effectively.

Drawing on its work with senior female executives, executive coaching firm Praesta Partners has found that taking time to reflect on your working life, and where you are going – often following illuminating feedback from a 360-degree process or from appraisal – frequently leads to a realization that the competence and ability that have helped you in your development so far won't take you much further[4] and that you need to "change gear" to maintain your progress. This realization in turn leads to a recognition that you must identify and understand the patterns of behavior that may be keeping you in that lower gear, and hindering you in your attempts to move up to the next leadership level.[5]

© Barbara Shore

MIND THE GAP!

If the next leadership level is board level, examples of patterns of personal behavior that have worked well previously, but won't any more, include acting and speaking as if what is right and wrong, or correct and incorrect, in a given situation is as clear to everyone else, as it is to you; failing to make connections with people; and issuing instructions, rather than soliciting views. These kinds of behaviors may have served you well in an operational role, but they will not be appropriate or effective behaviors on a board, irrespective of whether you're an executive or a non-executive director. The board is an altogether more subtle place.

Deciding to change

To bring some of the above points to life, let's look at the case of a client who realized, after receiving some tough feedback, that she needed to do some serious thinking about herself.

She was two levels below the board of a FTSE 100 company, and being groomed as a director, when her HR director approached us and asked whether we would be willing to work with her. She had an MBA, just the right kind of experience for the board, including several years of operational experience in the US, impressive technical skills, a good grounding in strategy and was highly regarded in the company. The HR director described her as an excellent hard-nosed negotiator; driven and very smart. Her Achilles' heel was her lack of emotional intelligence.

She was very good at managing "up" and all right, but not great, at peer-to-peer relationships. Her weakness was people skills with her team and other subordinates. Her strong and, in most respects, admirable task focus was coupled with a hard-driving approach and an absence of human warmth. The HR group director had recently told her that this lack of warmth and affinity with others would hold her back. She had a five-year plan for her career, culminating in her appointment to the board, but he had felt obliged to explain that, although her "weakness" wouldn't prevent her from gaining the next promotion, it would prevent her from gaining the one after that – getting on to the board. So she needed to work on her style, people skills and "leadership polish" if she was serious about getting on to the board.

As you can imagine, this wasn't welcome news for this able and very successful executive, and she initially recoiled from it. But after letting the unwelcome, but enlightening feedback "sit" for a couple of weeks, she accepted the information she'd been given and resolved to address the problem it had revealed. In her typically systematic way, she began by digging deeper into the causes of her weakness and then set about working on changing her behavior.

Getting yourselves together

You can't change your behavior at will. It is not just a matter of adding a skill, plugging a gap in an instrumental way or going on a course. You must first understand why you behave in that particular way before you can give yourself good reasons to behave, operate or exert influence in a different way. Thinking about these things may lead on to the deep reflection we referred to earlier – a curiosity about yourself; a wish to explore whether the road you have chosen is providing, or is likely to provide, what you really want; if your developing career is compatible with other life roles that are also important to you; how you can draw more on your full, not just your working, self to develop a more authentic style of leadership.

The term "individuation" was coined by the psychologist, Carl Jung, to describe that stage in a person's life (more often in the second half of life, although it can occur earlier) when he or she begins to look for, or stumble towards, a reconciliation or integration of the various aspects of his or her personality, to become that which he or she most truly is. Jung saw the process as consisting partly of conflict management and partly of collaboration:

> Conscious and unconscious do not make a whole when one of them is suppressed and injured by the other. If they must contend, let it at least be a fair fight with equal rights on both sides. Both are aspects of life. Consciousness should defend its reason and protect itself, and the chaotic life of the unconscious should be given the chance of having its way too – as much of it as we can stand. This means open conflict and open collaboration at once. That, evidently, is the way human life should be.[6]

Achieving individuation often involves deep change, and deep shifts in outlook. Herminia Ibarra described the basic process in her book *Working Identity*:

> Small choices accumulate within a harder-to-change framework of ingrained habits, assumptions, and priorities. But after a while, the old frames start to collapse under the weight of new data. Sooner or later, the cumulative force of the small steps we have been taking requires a more profound change in the underlying framework of our lives.[7]

Participation in the FTSE 100 Cross-Company Mentoring Programme can help trigger, in some mentees, the "more profound change" Professor Ibarra describes. Let us hear from two of them, in their own words:

> When you are in a senior executive role, especially with international commit-ments, you can be called to attention 24/7. Taking time out to reflect on yourself can be a luxury, whereas in fact you must see it as a necessity if you want to take yourself seriously and to be taken seriously as a director. I was fortunate enough

to have the opportunity to receive very broad, 360-degree feedback. There were some pleasant surprises in there and also some pointers for more work. I was able to take time out to look at some of the root causes of how people were perceiving me and, as a result of this work, I am now a much broader person. (group executive, FTSE 100 engineering company)

Working on the feedback has taught me not to make everything task focused. I understand more now about the importance of networking, not feeling it is a waste of time. Another insight was the need for me to create "me time"; to focus on how I actually came across to others. I do this now. So I confront less, I have a broader sense of myself, and I am a more rounded, happy person. (company secretary, FTSE 100 manufacturing company)

The bigger picture

As we suggested in Chapter 4, moving on to a board is a step change – the point at which the skills, qualities, attributes and approaches you have and are accustomed to use, although they remain necessary, cease to be sufficient. Moving from the vertical to the horizontal element of the T-piece requires an intellectual strength certainly; but efficiency at the task and straightforward problem-solving are not enough. The next stage requires the executive to be comfortable with ambiguity and strategy – people who excel at the tactical and operational sometimes struggle with the strategic – as well as an ability to encourage and inspire, and deal in the fuzzier and less rational currencies of mission, vision and values.

Those to whom these qualities don't come naturally, or who have had no occasion until now to try to acquire them, should look for them within themselves. Leadership is not something you "put on," like a raincoat. Its emergence in an individual is usually accompanied by a growing interest in the world beyond the organization; an opening of the mind, a wish to see the bigger picture. This is why chairmen and CEOs organize board retreats or awaydays. They seek unfamiliar environments for their high-level discussions, because when you're "out of the box" physically, it's much easier to get out of the box mentally. We think more deeply and more widely when there's less to remind us of the normal and conventional.

Be thoughtful; develop your empathy; talk to people you don't normally talk to and try to walk in their moccasins; imagine how you would think and what you would do in their situations; broaden the scope of your speculation beyond your own experience. If you keep thinking what you've always thought and doing what you've always done, you'll not only get what you've always got, you will also be who you've always been.

Authenticity

The goal of this process of deep reflection (working alone, or with an experienced professional) is Jung's goal of individuation; the unlocking of the person you truly are, and the gradual assimilation by that person, as you become comfortable with her, of your working persona to create your own unique leadership style. That is what we mean by "authenticity." Several contemporary writers on leadership have emphasized the importance of authenticity as a leadership quality.[8] People want to work with and be led by "real people," who "live" their values and wear the full colors and textures of their personalities on their sleeves.

When senior executives work with us or people like us, they usually achieve a number of breakthrough insights. One of the most striking (and often most surprising) is the sudden realization that, somehow or other, they've acquired a persona they use exclusively for work; one which they have unconsciously developed to fit what they see as the essentially rational world of management. It is usually colder, more impersonal and less sensitive than the personae they deploy as father, mother, sibling or friend. With this insight, comes the realization that perhaps they would enjoy work more and become more effective and influential, if they were *more themselves at work.*

In an earlier book based on interviews with 52 women leaders,[8] one of the authors found that a distinctive characteristic of the women who had been interviewed was that they deployed their personal qualities and attributes as *skills*, meaning that who they were, as people, was a fundamental part of how they behaved, as leaders. Cooper and Sawaf have described this approach as "putting integrity to work."[9] When women find themselves operating in environments where they are unable, or find it hard, to put who they are – their integrity – to work, they feel unwelcome in the organizational culture.

Some women try to conceal the feminine sides of their personalities in what they perceive as the incorrigibly masculine environments at the top of large organizations, and so deny to themselves, to their colleagues and to their organizations, all the creativity and power of an authentic, fully deployed personality.

Our work with many senior executives has convinced us that successful leaders are adept at gaining access to and deploying the aspects of their personalities that will be most appropriate for the people or situations at hand. You obviously can't acquire this skill without really understanding yourself. If you put on and shrug off personae that are fabricated or artificial, in the sense that they are not authentic aspects of your personality

– not really "you" – you will come across as insincere, as "play-acting." Deep reflection, insight and the development of self-awareness are the only routes to unlocking your full repertoire of authentic personae and developing the ability to attract, influence and inspire others, and thus become not only an effective and influential leader, but also a fulfilled human being.

Reflection tips

We end this chapter with a few pointers to help you on your journey of self-discovery.

1. *Get feedback*
    - From others: to develop a picture of your strengths and weaknesses, ask those who know you well for feedback about your impact on them, and what changes in your style and approach would make a beneficial difference.

    - From tools: tools such as Johari's Window or the Myers–Briggs Type Indicator (you will need an accredited practitioner to help with this) can provide useful insights, or at least food for thought. If your company offers personal profiling, as part of its executive development program, take it up.

2. *Find a trusted "learning partner" colleague*
    Find someone you really trust at work, with whom you can talk about your personal development objectives. Ask for their help in giving you day-to-day supportive and challenging feedback. Ask: How did I come across? What's better? What still needs to improve?

3. *Get an executive coach*
    Ask your company to demonstrate how much it values you by investing in a course of coaching to help you achieve your full potential and use the coach to help you focus on your self-development; to design experiments to boost your confidence and skill; to help you to find new ways to look at the situations you face; to help you see inside yourself; and to support and challenge you in your learning.

4. *Find a mentor*
    Find someone outside your immediate work situation who has "been there and done it" (whatever the "it" is that you are trying to do) and persuade him or her to become your adviser. Your mentor's status, experience and independence will allow you to discuss your develop-

ment in confidence, weigh up alternative scenarios, learn the unwritten rules and avoid mistakes.

5. *Understand your own background*
   Explore the main events that have shaped your life, and deepen your understanding of how they affect how you are today. What events had the most profound impact on you? What were the emotional highs (and lows)? How have they affected the way you see the world and how you respond to people and situations?

6. *Review your personal portfolio*
   Notice how you behave in the different areas of your life – how are you with family, friends? In what ways are your social and domestic personae similar to and different from your work persona? If the differences are significant, what steps could you take to achieve greater integration, in ways that would benefit both?

7. *Actively experiment*
   Take risks by changing the way you habitually do things. Be willing to move out of your comfort zone – you will not develop unless you do. For example, share more of yourself, your wants, your concerns, your fears; notice your impact on others, and what it feels like to do this.

References

1. *Plato*, Apology, 38a.
2. *Faster Faster*, Heather Dawson, Praesta Partners, 2007.
3. *Resonant Leadership*, Richard Boyatzis and Annie McKee, Harvard Business School Press, 2005.
4. *What Got You Here Won't Get You There*, Marshall Goldsmith with Mark Reiter, Hyperion, 2007.
5. *Personal and Organisational Transformation*, Dalmar Fisher and William R. Torbert, McGraw-Hill, 1995.
6. *An Introduction to Jung's Psychology*, Frieda Fordham, Penguin, 1991.
7. *Working Identity: Unconventional Strategies for Reinventing Your Career*, Herminia Ibarra, Harvard Business School Press, 2003.
8. *The Changing Culture of Leadership: Women Leaders' Voices*, Elizabeth Coffey, Clare Huffington and Peninah Thomson, The Change Partnership, 1999.
9. *Executive EQ: Emotional Intelligence in Business*, Robert Cooper and Ayman Sawaf, Orion Business Books, 1997.

CHAPTER 9

Board games

You need to consider how to develop and position yourself to create options for the future. Every new commitment needs to add breadth and depth and, with it, additional skills, experience, interests, opportunities and relationships. Unless and until you get involved, no one will ever think of you.

Sir Rob Margetts, chairman, Legal & General plc

Orr was crazy, and could be grounded. But, because the rules said "a concern for one's safety in the face of dangers that were real and immediate was the process of a rational mind," Orr would cease to be crazy as soon as he asked to be grounded, and would thus have to fly more missions. Orr would be crazy to fly more missions and sane if he didn't, but if he was sane, he had to fly them. If he flew them, he was crazy and didn't have to; but if he didn't want to, he was sane and had to. Yossarian was moved deeply by the absolute simplicity of this inescapable dilemma and let out a respectful whistle. "That's some catch, that Catch-22," he observed. "It's the best there is," Doc Daneeka agreed.[1]

We suggested in Chapter 4 that Nomcos on the lookout for directors usually seek candidates who have, among other things, authenticity and leadership qualities. The catch, for women, is that most people associate leadership qualities with male traits, and if they assume or adopt male traits, they may be seen as lacking authenticity. Their dilemma is similar to Orr's. They can adopt male traits and tick the leadership quality box, but as soon as they do, they compromise their chances of ticking the authenticity box.

A second double bind, which applies to men as well as women (but is amplified for women by the first), is that Nomcos on the lookout for directors normally favor candidates who have board experience. The catch is obvious – if you don't have board experience, you can't become a director, and if you don't become a director, you can't gain board experience. (Baroness Fritchie, the former commissioner for public appointments in the UK, likened the catch for women to actors who need an equity card to act, but can't get an equity card without first acting.)

Fortunately, this catch is not as awesomely simple or inescapable as catch-22. We know this, because although the crazies in Yossarian's war were never grounded, women have become directors. Not many, it's true (and not enough in our view), but a growing number of women are somehow extricating themselves from the double binds, and getting on the boards of our largest companies.

We discussed some strategies for extricating yourself from the first "perception" double bind in Chapter 4. We focus, in this chapter, on how to escape the second.

Gaining board-like experience

We noted in Chapter 2 that an important quality of the main board of a listed company, which distinguishes it from the board of an unlisted or subsidiary company, for example, is that in addition to being at the top of the organization, it's also on the edge. It's the primary interface between the organization and the outside world; the "face of the organization" for customers, investors, capital markets, the law, regulators, local communities and the general public. It is, in a sense, the personification of the organization.

Civil society is full of board-like groups of men and women who hold the reins of power in, and represent to the outside world, literally thousands of organizations, ranging from parishes, schools, clubs and not-for-profits, to hospitals, quangos, political parties and trades unions. The organizations under their governance vary enormously, of course, in their size and type; their purposes and objectives; their assets and resources; the legislation and regulations to which they are subject; and the number and nature of their members, stakeholders and constituencies.

But they share certain common features. They're all right at the top of their organizations. They all have a legal or quasi-legal status conferred on them by laws, constitutions or articles of association. Their conduct, when they meet, is always governed by conventions and formalities, such as agendas, motions, votes and the special, *primus inter pares* (first among equals) status of the "chair," with its casting vote.

By and large, positions within the governing groups of virtually all these myriad organizations that give substance to civil society are open to both genders and it goes without saying that landing a top executive from a large company would be a major coup for practically all of them.

A case in point

Britain's NHS has recently sent out a call to people with "proven commercial skills" to apply for the positions of non-executive directors of new business units being formed within all NHS Trusts.

The letter to the organizers of the FTSE 100 Cross-Company Mentoring

Programme from a member of the NHS Appointments Commission, which is keen to correct the gender imbalances on many existing Trust boards, said that joining an NHS Trust board "would allow you to gain unique governance experience," and pointed out that NHS Trusts have budgets of £400–500 million, "which is the equivalent of a FTSE 350 company." Other suggested advantages for becoming a NED in the NHS are:

■ The appointments are made in the areas where applicants live, so there are no long journeys to board meetings

■ It's "a fantastic networking opportunity that will enable you to build relationships with senior executives from all walks of life in your local community"

■ It will "extend your learning ... and develop new skills that can be transferred back into your workplace"

■ It will provide an "opportunity to contribute to the success of the economy in the town or city in which you live"

■ It will give you a say in "locally made decisions" and "allow you to put something back into your local community"

■ "During maternity leave, or an extended career break ... [it] will allow you to continue to use your skills and experience ... [and] maintain your involvement with a business environment during your absence."

Whether or not you agree with the correspondent that this latest NHS reorganization is a "major CV opportunity" (we'll come to that in a moment), the case is well made. These are the kinds of advantages that NED positions in the NHS, and other similar, non-corporate organizations, can offer. Such appointments are relevant, in the sense that they can provide experience analogous, if not equivalent, to serving as a main board director, and they will normally be seen as such by those separating the CV-wheat from the CV-chaff.

But for those looking for opportunities to serve on these boards and board-like groups, there are literally thousands to choose from, and in taking up one of them, you will incur an opportunity cost in the form of the hundreds of others you cannot, therefore, take up. The term "opportunity cost" is defined, by economists, as "the next best opportunity foregone." Since you can't take up all opportunities, you have to be sure that the opportunity you do take up is the best that is available in the circumstances, given your interests and goals.

Selected experience

Opinions differ, among the chairmen and CEOs on the FTSE 100 Cross-Company Mentoring Programme, about how useful these kinds of experiences are. Most say they're excellent experience, and important credentials on CVs. (One chairman recently described the efforts that he and his mentee were making to obtain a FTSE 100 main board position as a "two-hop process," where the first hop was onto a non-FTSE 100 board.)

Many headhunters take the same view – when using clients' briefs to screen potential candidates, they need to be able to tick the board experience box.

But some mentors are wary about their mentees taking up NED appointments that seem too remote from the critical path to a FTSE 100 board. For them, the opportunity costs loom too large. One said that, although serving on the board of a charity could be good for contacts, mentees should take care to pick the right charity, and should not waste their time on a small charity or an NHS board "which won't expand your contacts." These two apparently opposing views can be reconciled by taking into account industry-specific experience and timing.

Industry criteria

Serving on an NHS Trust board could be useful, if the candidate is aiming at a NED position on a major pharmaceutical or healthcare company, or any company that counts the NHS among its customers. Her contacts would be usefully expanded and the experience she would gain would be seen by her target companies as very valuable.

Our advice, when selecting opportunities to gain board or board-like experience, is to ask yourself the following questions:

- Will it be interesting?

- Will I be able to make a significant contribution?

- Will it usefully expand my contacts?

- Will it give me insights into my target sectors?

- Will it enable headhunters to tick the "board experience" box?

- Will it contribute significantly to my long-term goals?

- Will it be practical, in terms of time commitments?

To help you to choose between opportunities, when more than one present themselves, and to assess their respective opportunity costs, it may be useful to give what appears to you to be an appropriate weighting to each question, and rank the opportunities accordingly.

Timing considerations

Did you hear the one about the woman who was driving to Taunton, and got lost? She stopped in open country and asked a local the way. "Oo, ah, mum," he said gloomily, chewing on a blade of grass. "If oi were goin' to Taunton, oi wouldna start from 'ere."

If a FTSE 100 main board is your planned destination, don't get lost on the way. When selecting intermediate goals and positions, bear in mind the risk that, if you choose anything but the best opportunity, you could find yourself in a cul-de-sac, or in open country far from your critical path. Plan your career. Put your planned route in your SatNav before you leave home, put your SatNav on your dashboard and resist any temptation to stray from the critical path. If you wait until you're halfway through your journey to plan your route, you're bound to make wrong turns.

You have to start from where you are, of course, but as soon as you've decided to engage, you should try to ensure that every move you make brings you closer to your goal. Gain operational experience as soon as you can; gain international experience too (small and medium-sized businesses going international will often look for a NED who knows foreign markets, cultures and work practices); and (our mentors keep saying this) don't stay in functional roles too long. They are often culs-de-sac.

Men seem to be better at this than women. They're much more focused on their goals; more dedicated to equipping themselves with the bits and pieces of experience that will strengthen their CVs; less easily attracted away from their critical path; and more willing to move out of their comfort zones. They're not intrinsically better, but they seem to be better at keeping their eyes on the target. (They also seem to be better at keeping the eyes of others on their targets – see below on headhunters.)

Whether or not a move is wrong, in terms of your ultimate goal, will depend in part on when you make it. Moves that make sense relatively early in your career won't make sense later on. As time passes, the number of good opportunities to gain board, or board-like, experience will diminish. Becoming a school governor or a NED of a small charity will be useful experience that will help to fill gaps (see Chapter 8) and prepare you for more challenging intermediate positions when you're still relatively young and inexperienced. But as you approach your goal, you may need to acknowledge that you've got from, and given to, such roles as much as you can; that you need to gain experience from more challenging, higher profile positions, more appropriate for your age and experience, and more similar to the FTSE 100 main board position you're aiming for.

USE THE ROAD MAP!

To put it simply, you need to upgrade the NED positions you take on progressively as your career develops – to move up from the FTSE 500 through the FTSE 350, to the FTSE 100, so to speak. It doesn't have to be a FTSE anything, of course. Our point here is that the quality and stature of the NED positions you seek, whether with a company, a charity, a public sector body, a private equity fund or some other organization, should be appropriate for your age, experience and the stage you have reached in your progress toward your goal.

Haunt the hunters

As you move up through your company hierarchy and, more generally, up into the board milieu and thence to the board candidate space at its centre, your searching strategies for board and board-like positions will change.

In the early stages, after your decision to engage, when your need is for relatively low-grade positions, you're on your own. So keep your eyes peeled, your ear to the ground and your antennae up and active. Network with your friends and colleagues both at work and within the local community where you live. Make it known that you're interested in the institutions of civil society, that you're willing to "serve" – we rather like that American term with its connotations of altruism and civic duty – and that you have much to contribute.

As your career progresses, you travel further along the road to your goal and you search for higher grade board and board-like experience, the market in positions appropriate for the stage you have reached becomes more organized. Companies and other organizations with board and board-like vacancies are still the buyers of your services, but for these higher ticket positions, where bad appointments can damage reputations and share prices, most large organizations manage these risks by employing executive search consultants, or "headhunters," as they are more commonly known.

Headhunters are vitally important intermediaries in the markets for both executive and non-executive board and board-like positions. To discuss, as we have done in this book so far, how to reach your goal of a FTSE 100 board position without mentioning headhunters is like playing Hamlet without the prince. You need to sign up with the headhunters, particularly with those specializing in NED positions. Get to know them. Make sure that they are all aware of your interest and credentials and have the full version of your CV on file. Send them the entire new version whenever you update it.

Above all, *keep in touch*. A headhunter told us that one of the most striking differences between men and women looking for NED positions is that after the initial meeting to discuss the aspiring director's preferences and credentials, men are usually much more diligent than women about keeping in touch. Because they're more focused on their goals (see above), they call every two weeks or so to ask whether any interesting possibilities have come up, pop in for a chat if they're passing, and generally take pains to keep themselves in the forefront of the headhunter's mind. You can overdo this and get to be a pain, but confining your contacts with headhunters to a Christmas card is just as bad. You will give the impression that you are merely "going through the motions"; that you don't want it enough. Your name will, therefore, be unlikely to spring to the headhunter's mind when she or he receives new instructions from a client about a position that may be perfect for you.

Make the most of it

This might seem a statement of the blindingly obvious, but once you are on a board, don't rest on your laurels and on the tick inside the board experience box. Make the most of it. Be active; contribute; undertake projects; make your presence felt. Your co-directors are part of your network now. They will talk about you to their networks, including their headhunters, and may feel inclined later on, if they're sufficiently impressed by your qualities, abilities and commitment, to recommend you for other higher status NED positions.

Don't be tempted to regard your first board position as a reward for all your networking and hard work and start to coast. Your journey's not over. Active and strong-willed NEDs can get a lot done, and make a significant contribution to the success of their companies and the wellbeing of society at large.

Anna Ford was appointed a NED of J Sainsbury plc in May, 2006. She had no retail experience, but having been a newscaster and a current affairs journalist since 1974, she was seen to have a wider outlook than most retailers on national and international affairs, and to be of an independent mind, capable of challenging the board.

A year after her appointment to the board, she was asked to chair the corporate responsibility committee, which works to ensure that the company:

- is best for food and health

- is sourcing with integrity

- has respect for our environment

- makes a positive difference to the community

- is a great place to work.

Anna has co-hosted, with Sainsbury's CEO Justin King, six dinners to which some 50 members of relevant organizations and the public, some of whom were experts in their own fields, were invited to talk about how Sainsbury could improve corporate responsibility policies.

Thanks partly to the series of dinners and other work carried out by Ms. Ford's corporate responsibility committee, Sainsbury received the award for the best corporate responsibility report of the year.

Reflections for companies

Organizations have a number of adaptive opportunities here:

- They can review their lists of essential credentials for board candidates, so that there's a better fit between positions and candidates of both genders

- They can try to ensure that their most able female executives do not drift too early in their careers into pink collar functions

- They can help them to cut their teeth on the boards of subsidiaries, encourage them to apply for external NED positions and use their own networks to keep watch for suitable NED vacancies for them.

Company leaders often say they can't find senior women to appoint to their boards – that there don't seem to be enough suitably qualified women around. That's very encouraging as far as it goes. At least it means they're looking for them. But it is vexing for ambitious women (and men) when those same company leaders say they can't spare their senior executives; that their time is too valuable to the company to allow them to spend it on potentially time-consuming outside jobs.

Thankfully, this kind of beggar-thy-neighbor attitude seems to be dying out. There's a growing recognition that a NED appointment can be a valuable part of executive development and an important tool of talent management.

In an article in the *Sunday Times* in 2006, Roger Eglin reported that HR departments in large UK companies were helping their rising stars find NED appointments at smaller companies so that "they can broaden their experience" and also because, if they didn't, "they run the risk that talented young executives will go elsewhere."[2]

Eglin talked to Reg Sindall, group HR director at retailer, GUS (the owner of Argos and Homebase), who said:

> Non-executive positions are a win for everyone. Smaller companies get the expertise of a top executive and this is a superb way of broadening a director's skills and motivation. They can be far more hands-on and feel they are making a difference in a smaller company in a way that would be difficult to achieve in a large one.

Before joining GUS, Sindall had been HR director at Bass, the brewing group, which appoints "internal" non-execs; senior people just below board level who sit on the boards of subsidiary companies.

Denise Jagger, a partner of the law firm, Eversheds, told Eglin that when she was an executive director of Asda, the UK supermarket group owned by US retailing giant, Wal-Mart, all Asda executive directors were encouraged to hold NED positions, "because this allowed them to develop a broad business perspective." Jagger herself was a NED of Scarborough Building Society while she was at Asda, and is on the board of SCS Upholstery, plus a number of charities. She recalled:

> I certainly learnt many new skills, which I brought back to Asda. It broadened my horizons and kept me at Asda for longer.

NED positions are "a win for everyone," as Reg Sindall said. Company leaders should recognize that and, as the ratio of executive to non-executive directors increases in favor of the latter on the average board, it should become routine for them to swap people from their "marzipan" layers (just below the board) with each other to serve as NEDs on their respective boards.

References

1. *Catch-22*, Joseph Heller, Simon & Schuster, 1961.
2. Roger Eglin, "The new breed of non-exec takes off," *Sunday Times*, January 29, 2006.

CHAPTER 10

Over the horizon

The FTSE 100 Cross-Company Mentoring Programme is beginning to have an impact upon the rate of appointment of women to senior executive and non-executive roles in the UK. There is more to do, of course, but this innovative, business-to-business initiative is delivering results.

Sir John Parker, chairman, National Grid plc

This book is based mostly on what we've learned from the mentors and mentees who have actively participated in the FTSE 100 Cross-Company Mentoring Programme and from our own experiences as leaders of the program. Insofar as it describes the program and what we and the participants have learned from it, it should, therefore, be seen as a snapshot of the position in early 2008 when the program had been running for a little over three years.

As we explained in Chapter 1, the program is evolving more or less constantly. It's a work in progress. So we thought it might be interesting, for the reader, to conclude with an account of what the program's participants and organizers were thinking at the time of writing about where the program was and should be going in future.

We will begin with a summary of the discussion at what amounted to a brainstorming session in London towards the end of 2007, go on to suggest one way to maintain the momentum of recent progress towards a better gender balance on the boards of large companies and then end the book with some speculative thoughts about prospects for globalizing cross-company mentoring.

The Hoare's bank brainstorm

At a dinner in October 2007 at C. Hoare & Co., the 335-year-old independent private bank at 37 Fleet Street in London, the future of UK company boards and the FTSE 100 Cross-Company Mentoring Programme were discussed. Bella Hopewell, the family-owned bank's second "lady partner" and a strong supporter of the program, was our host for the evening.

As paintings of Hoare partners, from the seventeenth century to the present day, looked on, the program's leaders asked the guests, mentors, mentees and search consultants to address the three components of the question: what more can search consultants, chairmen and CEOs, and women eager to secure board appointments do to help increase the number of female directors on the boards of our largest companies?

Since it's extremely rare, to say the least, for the three groups of people implicated in, and affected by, the gender imbalance on boards to face each other across any kind of table, we thought it would be worthwhile making notes of the proceedings and summarizing the answers that emerged for each of the three groups mentioned in the question. The informal and open exchange was specifically designated as being under the Chatham House Rule, which states that:

> participants are free to use the information received, but neither the identity nor the affiliation of the speaker(s), nor that of any other participant, may be revealed.

What more can search consultants do?

Several guests felt that the search consultants should search more deeply and more widely in their quests for suitable female candidates. They should:

- Go down one or two levels below the main board

- Look not only at the executive committees of FTSE 350 companies, but also at the level below the executive committees of larger FTSE companies

- Broaden their search to overseas subsidiaries to find women board candidates of different nationalities. One guest suggested: "You need to expand your networks beyond the UK to find women for global boards."

It was felt that some search consultants tended to take too much as read, the briefs they are given by company chairmen looking for NEDs. They should challenge the criteria put forward by chairmen for NED positions and help them to think out of the box about what they really need. Said one guest, "If the criteria you're given are too tight, you should consider offering a 'surprising' candidate."

A related suggestion was that search consultants should question whether it was always essential for a candidate to have "P&L" (profit and loss), that is, operational, experience, and should point out to clients, for example, that executives from functional roles, many of whom are female, may have wider skills and outlooks than operational managers, which could enrich the board's collective competence.

Search consultants could also, it was suggested, help women in general, and the program mentees in particular, to understand how appointments are made by:

■ Teaching them "how to play the game"

■ Demystifying the process

■ Spelling out how candidates should behave. One mentee said, "Perhaps we need to present our experiences and skills differently, but to do that effectively, we need to know what skills and experience you're looking for."

Several guests thought that search consultants could help mentees to understand the role of the board better. One chairman suggested they could "help mentees to understand the role of the NED; that it's not just about operational issues." It was widely felt that search consultants could "manage mentees' expectations better, give them honest feedback and work with them to identify their strengths."

It was suggested that all search consultants involved in board appointments should:

■ Have access to an up-to-date list of mentees on the FTSE 100 Cross-Company Mentoring Programme

■ Get to know the potential women candidates

■ Become their advocates

■ Consult with each other (that is, across search firms) about who might have a relevant assignment to suit any of the mentees

■ Introduce to mentors on the FTSE 100 Cross-Company Mentoring Programme any really good women they come across, and suggest that they be considered for future posts. Said one chairman, "Trust the system [the mentoring program] enough to say it's a good pool; that it's worth meeting the people in it."

One guest suggested the search consultants should challenge the practice of medium-sized plcs (FTSE 250/350 firms) of relying on their networks to find NEDs for their boards, and put appropriate mentees forward as candidates to FTSE 250 chairmen.

What more can chairmen and chief executives do?

Several guests suggested that, if, as one chairman said (and another concurred), "75 percent of the time P&L experience is the 'feed' for an NED role," chairmen and CEOs should try to give their women managers P&L experience earlier on in their careers.

Another chairman suggested that he and his fellow chairmen should

> review how we assess P&L. We should use the broadest possible definition; accountability for a whole entity, for example. This includes being responsible for a cost centre. In other words [we say] that suitable NED candidates have to be in a position where they can identify with the executive. Maybe we could broaden out the definition [of P&L] to business leadership, that is, running a whole business.

Mentors were also urged to test their assumptions about what mentees do and could do, and be more open about their needs:

- Get them talking about what they do

- Help them to be realistic about what they can aspire to, and what a board does

- Explain what you need your board directors to do, in terms of expected tenure and time commitment, and how to behave.

Other mentees wanted to learn more from the chairmen and CEOs. "Tell us your stories; what you would do differently next time if you were seeking or undertaking your first NED role?" "Help us to understand the unwritten rules of the game."

In their relationships with search consultants, chairmen and CEOs were urged to:

- Recommend and push women with search consultants

- Generalize about women from successes, rather than failures

- Propose their own senior executives to other boards as NEDs.

It was felt by several guests that to get more women onto boards, CEOs and chairmen should "signal the need more strongly [to search consultants] that more needed to be done." They should give search consultants a clear brief about diversity. "You have to say that you want to see a diverse slate, otherwise it won't happen," said one mentee. Comments on similar lines included:

- Don't allow men-only lists of board candidates

- Ensure that there's at least one woman on every shortlist

- Be critical of the list provided by search consultants

- Define what you need for the board, in diversity terms

- Ask for something different; a woman, a mixed team, functional or ex-functional experience as opposed to plc board experience

- Be broadminded.

It was suggested that chairmen and CEOs could also do more to ensure that their organizations are accommodating for women. "Make sure that men don't trample over women in the boardroom," one mentee urged. Another said:

Ensure consistency between your view as chairman and the views of your CEO and other executives over issues such as the talent pipeline within the organization and wider attitudes to diversity.

A chairman suggested:

You should review human capital at board meetings and ask questions about where people are moving to next, and you should introduce your high potentials to your NEDs.

When describing how he handles human capital issues on the board, another chairman said:

Make sure the board's very thorough at talent development and succession planning. Ask questions. Ensure the process goes on.

Another chairman/mentor urged his peers to help

change the company culture and keep talking about the vision. Diversity and inclusion should be the second thing you talk about, as chairman, after health and safety. You should champion the removal of bias from attraction, recruitment, assessment and promotion. Champion flexibility. Create a shared vision. Encourage jobs to be redesigned. Talk about all these things as a chairman.

What more can women themselves do?

Mentee guests at the Hoare's bank dinner were urged by a chairman to "be realistic about your first NED appointment – not many men would aspire to a FTSE 100 directorship straightaway." Another chairman counselled realism too, but also advised mentees to be proactive and "screen the FTSE 350 for opportunities." Other tips from the top, so to speak, included:

- Know what you want, and go after it

- Be strategic. Focus on what you can offer, and where

- Think positively about your abilities. Mentees have got to sort out their unique selling points to find out where they would fit

- Identify what you can bring, and be the best

- Remember, your best advert is your peer group

- Wind the dial up, in terms of ambition, and don't worry about being seen to be pushy

- Don't try to be a man

- Don't focus on your career all the time.

One chairman was challenged strongly by the women on his table, when he said:

> Be aware of the need to get operational experience early in your career. You need to "opt in" in your early to late thirties. When you're offered a line job, don't say "no" and opt for HR instead.

One woman objected: "Isn't the type of opting-in you're talking about still in the old terms?"

Another chairman/mentor also impressed on mentees the need to take a long-term view: "Do things that do not seem immediately urgent – be lateral in your thinking." Another said:

> Develop clear objectives and be clear about whether you view becoming a NED in isolation or as a stepping-stone to a more senior executive role.

A search consultant said mentees also need to understand

> the nature of the deal. If there's a hostile bid [and some board positions will be up for grabs if it goes through], you have to get in there and do the long hours.

"Maintain contacts, keep your CV up to date and market yourself more effectively," said another chairman mentor. "Work on your CV and your story to demonstrate how your skills are relevant," said another. Mentees were also advised to "recognize the value of relationships and the importance of developing and managing your personal profiles, and network beyond the search firms."

Search consultants had several suggestions for mentees:

■ Deal honestly and professionally with search consultants. Some people don't return phone calls

■ Get to know the search consultants; they can be your advocates at court

■ Be open about your efforts to be appointed to a board.

More specifically on the third point, one search consultant urged mentees to:

> Make sure you have consulted your own chairman and that he's supportive. We recently put up a shortlist to a FTSE 250 chairman including two women, because he wanted diversity. But the chairmen of the women's companies were not supportive. It didn't reflect well on them, or on us.

A chairman echoed this point: "Negotiate beforehand with your boss, to be sure you have his support."

Mentees were also urged to be "brutally realistic about time commitments, and agree them with your company in advance." Another chairman mentor said:

> There's a big issue about the time involved being a NED, so you should look for a company the interests of which are congruent with those of your own company.

Once on a board, the mentees were advised to

> take the risk out – be better than good, because, if it's your first board, it's a risk for the chairman to appoint you.

Another chairman urged mentees to

> be careful and analyse the situation before you join a board. Something will go wrong, even with good people and good procedures. You are at reputational risk,

and you've got to be clear about the risk you're taking. So be clear when you meet him [the appointing chairman] that there is trust between you and he is able to defend you if things go wrong.

Encouraging others

Although not mentioned at the dinner, mentees and other senior female executives on or close to main boards have vital roles to play as trailblazers for other ambitious women.

Nearly all the mentees on the FTSE 100 Cross-Company Mentoring Programme are helping younger women to develop their careers. That's great. We think role models are very important and, as we said in our earlier book, senior women are role models for younger women, whether they welcome it or not. Ambitious young men are much better served than ambitious young women in this respect, because companies are awash with male role models. Because there are relatively few of them, senior women are more visible role models than their male peers and must spread themselves more thinly. But high-flying female executives only have so much time, and should not allow their wish to help younger women distract them from making a success of their own careers.

We would, therefore, like to suggest that those women executives who do have senior positions in large companies and organizations, and who want to do something to help, should commit themselves to doing three "good things" a year for young women who are eager to emulate their success. Good things could include:

- accepting invitations to speak at conferences about diversity and "how I made it"

- engaging the male establishment in a discussion about how to improve their organization's ability to attract and keep able and talented women

- identifying high potential women in organizations, seeking them out and taking them under their wings in one way or another.

However, the most significant contribution any senior woman can make over the medium to longer term is to focus her eyes on the prize and to devote sufficient time and energy to her own career to reach the board and, once there, to make a major impact. If the gender balance on the boards of our large companies is to keep moving in the right direction, the link between the number of women on a company's board and the company's performance must be strengthened by very effective female directors.

These are the role models that ambitious women need and the reasons why companies will appoint more female directors.

Towards a global network of programs

In a business world where everyone but the tax man is becoming blind to national borders, where French beans come from Kenya, cars come from Japan, a rapidly growing number of products of all kinds, from toys to electronic components, come from China, where IT and other support services are supplied from India, and no large company lacks a global strategy, a FTSE 100 Cross-Company Mentoring Programme will seem to some people unfashionably local, perhaps even parochial.

It's not as if the problem that the program's designed to address – the relative lack of women at the top of organizations – is peculiar to the UK. Women are underrepresented on corporate boards and in other leadership positions practically everywhere. In a global ranking of gender diversity at the top of large companies and organizations, the UK would be near the top – below the US and Scandinavian countries, but well above most central and southern European countries and more or less the rest of the world.

But we had to start somewhere and since the UK is where we are, the UK is where we started. We see ourselves as making connections with people in other countries working in this space. It is great to see companies and organizations in other countries taking up the baton and starting programs designed to do something positive about the lack of women on company boards. Representatives from the UK program and similar initiatives, either launched recently or mooted in France, Canada, Spain, Australia and the Netherlands, which were inspired by and are learning from the experience of the UK program, will be invited to an international colloquium on gender diversity on boards to be held in London in 2008. It will be hosted by the London Stock Exchange (LSE), courtesy of the LSE's CEO, Clara Furse.

There are three reasons why the globalization of the cross-company mentoring idea makes sense:

1. If UK companies are better run by men *and* women than by men *or* women, the same is surely true of companies in general, wherever they are based.

2. The number of non-UK leaders of FTSE 100 companies reflects the fact that the market in top management talent, including top female management talent, is global, and women seeking board positions, and companies seeking directors, should, therefore, be looking abroad, as well as at home.

3. The widespread recognition of the value of diversity in general, and gender diversity in particular in business, endows the female gender with a competitive advantage.

As we pointed out in Chapter 7, the appointment of a woman to a male-dominated board delivers two benefits at once; the woman's special expertise, and a contribution to gender diversity. By the same token, appointing a foreign woman to the board endows it, in addition, with a contribution to national or ethnic diversity goals.

Afterword

We set up the FTSE 100 Cross-Company Mentoring Programme because we felt frustrated and wanted to add some momentum and a new dynamic to the glacially slow progress toward gender-balanced boards at large UK companies. We felt that we had to do something and since helping senior executives to realize their full potential, and helping large companies to establish and achieve diversity goals is what we do, the program is what we have done and will continue to do as it evolves and adapts to changing circumstances and new opportunities.

The point is to *do something*.

Millions of men and women all over the world now believe that all of us would be better off if women had stronger voices in companies and the other organizations and institutions of civil society. Simply to believe that is not enough, however. The better gender balance among the leaders of our civil society, which so many of us wish for, cannot be achieved by a communal wringing of hands. We must all, in our own ways and in our own areas of work and expertise, actively contribute to bringing it about.

FTSE 100 Cross-Company Mentoring Programme

Mentoring Guidelines©

Praesta Partners LLP

January 2008

The High-level Mentoring Process

What is mentoring?

Powerful people have mentored others since the dawn of human history. Indeed, it has always been an important part of the passing of power and authority – and responsibility – down the generations. Even the word 'mentor' is more than two millennia old, being derived from the name of a character in Greek mythology.[1]

Those being mentored have gone by many names. They have been called protégés, disciples, charges, students, wards, apprentices and, more recently, 'mentees'. Throughout history, the essence of what mentors did remained straightforward. They guided their charges towards the development of their fullest potential, enabling those charges to become masters in their own right.

Today there are relatively few people who reach the top, whether in business, commerce, politics, the military, professions, the Church, sport or whatever, who do not acknowledge the guidance and good example set out for them by a mentor at some crucial stage in their development. Such people will tell you that in the main their mentors never set out to impart a particular, detailed skill set. Instead they focused on giving the sort of general guidance, firmly rooted in their own wisdom and experience, that enabled those they were mentoring to shape their own careers more adroitly and successfully.

It sounds simple, and in general it is. What follows is deliberately focused on high-level mentoring relationships and is intended to provide a general framework within which a new mentor may successfully begin his or her mentoring role. This is of course not just about what the mentor may do. Mentoring is a two-way process and in many respects the preparation for mentoring meetings which needs to be done by the person who is being mentored – let's call that person the 'mentee' for the purposes of this document – is even more important. It is the mentee who must be responsible for the management of the relationship with the mentor, not the other way about. Included later on, therefore, is a section on what the mentee should do to ensure the mentoring process confers most benefit.

What makes a mentoring relationship successful?

Unsurprisingly, like most relationships, this one works best where:

▷   Both parties genuinely want the relationship to work.
▷   The relationship is strong because it is based on mutual respect, openness, honesty and trust.
▷   The mentee has given serious, structured thought to what it is they wish to get out of the process and shares this openly.
▷   Both parties commit to an agreed amount of time – which of necessity has to be quite small when people close to the top of major organisations are involved[2] – to the process; and honour the commitments made.
▷   The mentor establishes at the start his/her willingness to share helpful experiences – which often means sharing some of the challenges as well as the crowning successes of the mentor's own life and career.

The mentee's role in making mentoring a success

As the senior partner in the relationship, it is for the mentor to spell out to the mentee what the basis of the relationship is to be. The five points in the section immediately above may well be the template for this, whether used in a conversation or a letter.

It is also up to the mentor to make clear, well ahead of a first meeting, his/her expectations of the preparation that the mentee needs to do. This is most important and should include the mentee:

▷   Thinking about her long-term development – what are the current goals and aspirations? Does that definitely include being a director? An executive director? A non-executive director?
▷   Trying to be clear about what personal success – for her – would look like. What would it entail? What are the parameters? What are the key steps towards directorship?
▷   Attempting to define what barriers to success she is able to identify now and in the mid-term.
▷   Thinking through what she would like to get out of the mentoring – in what ways might it be most helpful? Where should the focus be for best advantage?

▷ Deciding how she will evaluate what she gets out of the mentoring process.

Time spent on these aspects will produce real value for both parties. It is of course important in all this that the mentor does not accept all the output from the mentee's prior thinking at face value. Part of the process – and an important part – depends upon the mentor's willingness to challenge the mentee's views of her life and career, to test assumptions about goals (and barriers) and to stretch her thinking.

What are the attributes of a good mentor?

Obviously there are some skills which are important. These include:

▷ Being willing to conduct all conversations with the mentee under conditions of strictest personal confidence.
▷ Empathetic listening – understanding by mentally putting oneself in the other person's shoes.
▷ Being willing to share experiences and learning freely, as appropriate.
▷ Being willing to reflect and develop insights into the mentee's world – and being prepared to share these.
▷ Able to act as a sounding board on confidential and personal matters.
▷ Being able to challenge strongly but with tact and understanding.
▷ Being able to provide open and constructive feedback, as appropriate.
▷ Encouraging the mentee to take control of her own destiny – to find the courage to realise her full potential.

A good degree of self-awareness on the part of the mentor always makes the deployment of these skills easier.

Towards a successful start to mentoring

Ahead of the first mentoring meeting:

▷ Facilitate an exchange of some basic information – a CV or similar biographical material might well be sufficient – as part of the 'getting to know you' process. It is also helpful for the mentor to have a sheet of A4 with the mentee's responses to three questions:

1. Why I want to be on the FTSE 100 Cross-Company Mentoring Programme (exploring intent).
2. What I would like to get out of being on the programme (exploring aspiration).
3. First thoughts about what I would like to discuss with a mentor.

Then aim to get the scene-setting and 'admin.' items dealt with:

▷ Set the scene to achieve a level of comfort in talking to each other, ensuring a good informal atmosphere, privacy, comfortable seating, etc.

▷ Be clear at the outset about the length of the meeting and the number of times you can commit to meeting. Typically successful mentoring relationships are based on a minimum of four meetings per year of an hour or hour and half's duration.

▷ Restate what will make the relationship a successful one – openness, honesty, etc. (see previous points).

▷ Agree some ground rules about how meetings will be conducted. (This is an open, two-way process and may best be tackled by asking the mentee for her views and preferences.)

▷ Achieve a mutual understanding of what the mentee hopes for from the mentoring overall.

▷ Be clear at the end about timing (and if possible, a date) for the next meeting – and about whose job it is to pursue it.

▷ Be clear between all parties about the overall duration of the mentoring relationship. You may wish to set a review point to discuss whether the arrangement is working for both of you.

Then, plunging into the substance of it:

▷ The process is a conversational one and as senior partner the mentor should be prepared to take a lead, especially in the early stages of mutual confidence building.

▷ Check and understand the issues facing the mentee; and the aims/ ambitions she can describe, based on preparation she will have done.

▷ Focus on the mentee's most pressing concerns at the start and build a conversation around what steps she might take to underwrite her own success.

▷ Share your own perceptions, experiences, and knowledge as you best see them helping the development of the conversation.

▷ Try to get the mentee to identify actions for herself from these conversations (e.g. If that's the issue and you can see a way to possible resolution, what will you do now to achieve it?).

▷ Check occasionally to confirm mutual understanding and to ensure the right issues are in focus.

▷ If you as mentor have promised help in any way outside the meeting (and this is not obligatory!), make a note of what is required; and ensure both parties know what the communications channels are.

▷ Keep for future reference some brief aide-mémoire of key topics discussed.

▷ Enjoy the conversation: this should be a pleasant – even a fun – experience for both parties!

What the mentor gains from the experience

Mentoring *is* a two-way street and while the balance of gains is heavily weighted in favour of the mentee – that, after all, is the purpose of the relationship – there may nevertheless be some small gains for the mentor, which may be summarised as:

▷ The satisfaction of knowing that your wisdom and hard-won experience is being put to invaluable use with a new generation of senior people.
▷ The chance to 'put something back' into one's professional life and environment. (And what is put back in mentoring *is* important.)
▷ A development of new insights on the part of the mentor – a frequent and perhaps surprising outcome, but a welcome one.
▷ The chance to help put right the lamentable lack of women at the top of British business, banking and commerce.

Peninah Thomson
Praesta Partners LLP
January 2008

Notes

1. Guide, friend and faithful counsellor to Ulysses – though the goddess Athena stole his form when she accompanied (and presumably mentored!) his son Telemachus, during the latter's search for his father.

2. It is difficult to envisage anyone at the top of such an organisation being able to give more than 60-75 minutes three times per annum (say) to this activity.

Argyris, Chris (1960) *Understanding Organisational Behaviour.* Homewood, IL, The Dorsey Press.

Baddeley, Simon and James, Kim (1987) "Owl, fox, donkey or sheep: political skills for managers", *Management Education and Development,* **18**(1): 3-19.

BBC (2006) *Woman's Hour from Joyce Grenfell to Sharon Osbourne: Celebrating Sixty Years of Women's Lives.* London, John Murray.

Berle, Adolf (1959) *Power without Property: A New Development in American Political Economy.* New York, Harcourt Brace.

Berle, Adolph and Means, Gardiner (1933) *The Modern Corporation and Private Property.* New York, Macmillan.

Bird, Steve (2006) "The woman who shook the City," *Sunday Times*, October 26.

Boyatzis, Richard and McKee, Annie (2005) *Resonant Leadership.* Harvard Business School Press.

Brook, Lesley and Graham, Jacey (2005) "Managing the female talent pipeline," in *The Female FTSE Report.* Cranfield School of Management.

Burrell, Ian (2007) "Lorraine Heggessey: still searching for the X factor," *Independent*, November 5.

Byrne, John, (2007) "Women change the rules of business." BBC Radio 4, *Changing the Rules.*

Bryan, Lowell, Matson, Eric and Weiss, Leigh (2007) "Harnessing the power of informal employee networks," *McKinsey Quarterly.*

Cadbury Report (1992) *The Financial Aspects of Corporate Governance.*

Campbell, Alastair (2007) *The Blair Years: Extracts from the Alastair Campbell Diaries.* London, Hutchinson.

Catalyst (2004) *The Bottom Line: Connecting Corporate Performance and Gender Diversity.* New York.

Catalyst (2007) *Census of Women Board Directors of the Fortune 500.* New York.

Catalyst (2007) *Census of Women Board Directors, Corporate Officers, and Top Earners of the Fortune 500.* New York.

Catalyst (2007) *The Bottom Line: Corporate Performance and Women's Representation on Boards.* New York.

Coffey, Elizabeth, Huffington, Clare and Thomson, Peninah (1999) *The Changing Culture of Leadership: Women Leaders' Voices.* London, The Change Partnership.

Coleman, John, Cooper, Christopher, Linnecar, Robin et al. (2007) *Gravitas.* London, Praesta.

Coleman, John, Cooper, Christopher, Linnecar, Robin et al. (2007) *Constructing your CV.* London, Praesta.

Cooper, Robert and Sawaf, Ayman (1997) *Executive EQ: Emotional Intelligence in Business.* London, Orion Business Books.

Cope, Mick (2003) *Personal Networking: How to Make your Connections Count.* London, Pearson Education.

Coulson-Thomas, Colin, *Developing Directors, A Guidebook for Building an Effective Boardroom Team*, www.policypublications.com/developingdirectors. htm.

Cranfield University School of Management (2006) *The Female FTSE Report 2006.*

Cranfield University School of Management (2007) *The Female FTSE Report 2007.*

Cunningham, Jane and Roberts, Philippa (2006) *Inside Her Pretty Little Head: a New Theory of Female Motivation and What it Means for Marketing.* London, Marshall Cavendish.

Dawson, Heather (2007) *Faster Faster.* London, Praesta Partners.

DeLong, Thomas, Gabarro, John and Lees, Robert (2008)"Why mentoring matters in a hypercompetitive world," *Harvard Business Review.*

The Diversity Practice Ltd. and Katalytik Ltd. (2007) *Different Women, Different Places.* Surrey, Brown-Forman.

Eagly, Alice and Carli, Linda (2007) "Women and the labyrinth of leadership," *Harvard Business Review*, September.

Eagly, Alice and Carli, Linda (2007) *Through the Labyrinth: The Truth about how Women Become Leaders.* Harvard Business School Press.

Eglin, Roger (2006) "The new breed of non-exec takes off," *Sunday Times*, January 29.

Equal Opportunities Commission (2007) *The Gender Agenda.*

Fisher, Dalmar and Torbert, William (1995) *Personal and Organisational Transformation.* New York, McGraw-Hill.

Flett, Christopher (2007) *What Men Don't Tell Women about Business: Opening Up the Heavily Guarded Alpha Male Playbook.* New York, Wiley.

Fordham, Frieda (1991) *An Introduction to Jung's Psychology.* New York, Penguin.

Frankel, Lois (2004) *Nice Girls don't get the Corner Office.* New York, Warner Business Books.

Garratt, Bob (2003) *Thin On Top: Why Corporate Governance Matters.* London, Nicholas Brealey.

Garratt, Bob (2003) *The Fish Rots from the Head*, London, Profile Books.

Goldsmith, Marshall with Reiter, Mark (2007) *What Got you Here Won't Get you There*. New York, Hyperion.

Greenbury Report (1995) *On Directors' Remuneration*.

Hawkins, Peter and Smith, Nick (2006) *Coaching, Mentoring and Organisational Consultancy: Supervision and Development*. Maidenhead, Open University Press/McGraw-Hill Education.

Heffernan, Margaret (2004) *The Naked Truth: A Working Woman's Manifesto on Business and What Really Matters*. San Francisco, Jossey-Bass.

Heller, Joseph (1961) *Catch-22*. New York, Simon & Schuster.

Hembrock Daum, Julie and Cohen Norris, Julie (2007) *Cornerstone of the Board: Building a New Board – Lessons from Spinoffs*. Spencer Stuart.

Hempel Report of The Committee on Corporate Governance (1998).

Hewlett, Sylvia Ann (2007) *Off-Ramps and On-Ramps: Keeping Talented Women on the Road to Success*. Harvard Business School Press.

Higgs Review of the Role and Effectiveness of Non-executive Directors, The Combined Code on Corporate Governance, Financial Reporting Council.

Hurst, Greg (2007) "Ministers urge Brown to change leadership style as Tory poll lead slips," *The Times*, December 31.

Hutchings, Victoria (2005) *Messrs Hoare Bankers: A History of the Hoare Banking Dynasty*. London, Constable.

Ibarra, Herminia (2003) *Working Identity: Unconventional Strategies for Reinventing Your Career*. Harvard Business School Press.

Incomes Data Services *Executive Compensation Review*, published monthly.

Kets de Vries, Manfred, Korotov, Konstantin and Florent-Treacy, Elizabeth (2007) *Coach and Couch: The Psychology of Making Better Leaders*. Basingstoke, Palgrave Macmillan.

Kramer, Vicki and Konrad, Alison (2006) "How many women do boards need"? *Harvard Business Review*.

Lehman Brothers Centre for Women in Business, The (2007) *Innovative Potential: Men and Women in Teams*. London, London Business School.

McKinsey & Company (2007) *Women Matter. Gender Diversity, a Corporate Performance Driver*. McKinsey & Company.

McKinsey & Company (2008) *Room at the Top: Women and Success in UK Business*. McKinsey & Company.

Merlin, Bella (2007) *The Complete Stanislavsky Toolkit*. London, Nick Hem Books.

Michaels, Adian (2007) "Luxottica eyes top jobs for women," *Financial Times*, December 4.

Middleton, Julia (2007) *Beyond Authority*. Basingstoke, Palgrave Macmillan.

Pettier, Bruce (2001) *The Psychology of Executive Coaching: Theory and Application*. Hove, Brunner-Routledge.

Rogers, Carl (1961) *On Becoming a Person: A Therapist's View of Psychotherapy*. London, Constable.

Roth, Louise Marie (2006) *Selling Women Short: Gender and Money on Wall Street*. Princeton, NJ, Princeton University Press.

Shaw, Peter and Linnecar, Robin (2007) *Business Coaching: Achieving Practical Results through Effective Engagement*. Chichester, Capstone.

Smith, Adam (1776) *An Inquiry into the Nature and Causes of the Wealth of Nations*, London, Ward, Lock and Tyler.

Stone, Carole (2004) *The Ultimate Guide to Successful Networking*. London, Vermilion.

Sveiby, Karl-Erik (1997) *The New Organizational Wealth: Managing and Measuring Knowledge-based Assets*. San Francisco, Berrett-Koehler.

Sveiby, Karl-Erik and Lloyd, Tom (1987) *Managing Knowhow*. London, Bloomsbury.

Thomson, Peninah (2007) "Being on a board", in Mirella Visser and Annalisa Gigante (eds) *Women on Boards: Moving Mountains*, Condé-sur-Noireau, EPWN Women@WorkNo.8.

Thomson, Peninah (2007) "The FTSE 100 Cross-Company Mentoring Programme," in Thérèse Torris (ed.) *Mentoring: A Powerful Tool for Women*. Condé-sur-Noireau, EPWN Women@WorkNo.7.

Tribe, R. and Morrissey J. (eds) (2005) *Handbook of Professional Ethical Practice for Psychologists, Counsellors and Psychotherapists*. Hove, Brunner-Routledge.

Turnbull Report (1999) *Internal Control: Guidance for Directors on the Combined Code*.

Tyson Report on the Recruitment and Development of Non-Executive Directors (2003).

Vinnicombe, S., Burke, R., Singh, V. et al. (eds) (2008) *Women on Corporate Boards of Directors: Research and Practice*. Cheltenham, Edward Elgar.

Wark, Penny (2007) "With prejudice", *Times2*, May 22.

Wittenberg-Cox, Avivah and Maitland, Alison (2008) *Why Women Mean Business*. Chichester, Wiley.